THE ABSOLUTE SEVERITY OF ENVIRONMENT

THE ABSOLUTE SEVERITY OF ENVIRONMENT

Mastering Retention & Recidivism Prevention

NICKOLAS DEJARNETTE

Nickolas DeJarnette

VERSE

"Bad company, corrupts good character."
(1 Corinthians 15:33)

*I want to dedicate this book to my wife Suze
and our 6 children—Agapito, Nick Jr., Niko, RJ, Jonathan, and Zanne.*

*I pray that in reading this book, my wife may find answers she may have
been looking for, a new and profound respect for not just the survivor in
me, but also for the transformation I fought so hard to achieve for God,
her, and our children—along with insight, strength, encouragement and
hope that nothing will break us, and that "no weapon formed against [us,
our marriage, and our children] will prosper" (Isaiah 54:17).*

*I pray that our children not only learn intimate truths about their
father, but also gain wisdom for their individual journeys. I pray that
their faith be increased, their souls be encouraged, and their spirits filled
with gratitude and thanksgiving for the lives they've been given by God.*

*Lastly, I pray that—as a family—we come to better understand the
"Absolute Severity of Environment" for the purpose of continually being
aware of our environments, urgently seeking out "new-tritious"
environments, desperately remaining within nutritious environments,
relentlessly creating nutritious environments, and lovingly introducing
future generations to some of the most nutritious environments under the
sun and on God's green earth.*

I love you all.

"It is with great pleasure that I introduced you to Nick, a remarkable individual with a unique story and an unwavering determination to succeed against all odds. In the pages that follow, you will embark on a journey through the various rooms of opportunity that Nick has navigated with finesse, understanding, and a profound sense of gratitude.

I first had the privilege of meeting Nick at Jemal King's "'*Make Real Estate Real' Family Reunion*" event, an occasion teaming with energy and enthusiasm for the endless possibilities within the real estate industry. Amidst the bustling crowd, Nick stood out not only for his charisma but also for his genuine appreciation for the knowledge and insights shared during the event. It was during our conversation that Nick humbly presented me with an envelope, expressing his desire to compensate for the content he had consumed over the years.

Nick's gesture spoke volumes about his character—a real trait indeed. His understanding of reciprocity and his willingness to acknowledge the value of the resources he had utilized exemplify his commitment to personal growth and development. It is this quality that sets Nick apart and forms the foundation of his journey through the rooms of opportunity that lie ahead.

Throughout the pages of this book, you will discover Nick's innate ability to discern which rooms he needs to be in—a skill honed through adversity and cultivated through experience. From the corridors of education to the boardrooms of business, Nick navigates with purpose, driven by a keen understanding of the benefits each room offers and the opportunities they present.

But Nick's journey is not merely one of passive observation; rather, he actively seeks to engage with the key players within each room, recognizing the importance of building meaningful relationships and fostering connections that extend beyond surface-level interactions. By doing so, Nick not only adds value to these rooms but also positions himself as a trusted collaborator and contributor, essential traits for long-term success and sustainability.

However, Nick's journey is not without its challenges. Like any path worth traversing, he encounters obstacles along the way—setbacks, doubts, and moments of uncertainty. Yet, it is Nick's resilience and determination that enable him to persevere, to weather the storms and emerge stronger on the other side. His commitment to staying in the room, not just for days or months, but for years, speaks to his unwavering dedication to his goals and aspirations.

As you accompany Nick on his journey through the rooms of opportunity, I encourage you to reflect on your own path—the rooms you inhabit, the key players you engage with, and the value you bring to those spaces. For in Nick's story lies a universal truth—that with vision, perseverance, and a spirit of gratitude, we can all navigate the rooms of opportunity that await us. With warm regards,"

—Eric D Thomas, PhD
AKA - *ET THE HIP HOP PREACHER*

"Nickolas takes us on a journey to the darkest and most desperate corners of the world and leads us to enlightenment and the possibility of hope and promise for a new attainable way of life. Written with blood, sweat and tears, this book not only moves the reader through so many emotional experiences, but is truly so motivating and inspiring."

—Samya N. Yamin, Psy.D,
(Licensed Psychologist), Nick's Therapist

"Phenomenal! Nick has written a book that highlights a principle I deeply believe in. "Your level of exposure will determine your level of success!" The stories he shares testify that our lives shape out based on who we put ourselves around, what we believe in, what he calls our "internal environment," and where we allow ourselves to go. This is a must-read!"

—Jemal King, *The 9 to 5 Millionaire*
(Retired Police Officer), Financial Coach/Mentor of Nick

"Nick's journey has been heartbreaking, but his story is far more inspirational and serves as an example of the notion that one can change "their story" at any time in their life. Nick talks about environment and the importance of putting yourself in the best places to optimize growth, prosperity, and happiness. What is not explicitly written about, but surely comes through in the pages, is the story of resilience and the steadfast determination to always be pushing forward no matter the difficult circumstances you may find yourself in. Nick shows that you can come from the darkest parts of the world and turn your life into something of meaning and impact that ultimately brings light to so many. It's certainly not easy, especially when you are starting at an extreme disadvantage, but Nick provides the blueprint and proves that refusing to give up and continuing to get better a little every day does, in fact, create positive outcomes. Nick's no excuses attitude and radical accountability will come through with each chapter and should inspire all of us to take our destiny, happiness and prosperity into our own hands, anyone that thinks a better future isn't possible should consider this required reading."

—Chris Bright,
Founder and CEO of one of the Fastest Growing Private Companies in the US
(Inc. Magazine, 2023), Combat Veteran and Candidate for US Congress—Nick's Business Mentor

"Grace and peace in our world, there are great writers, poets & storytellers but every now and then we are graced with truth ambassadors, and with the stroke of his pen my brother Nickolas DeJarnette has been added to this list; the power of his testimony coupled with the relevancy of his transparency takes the reader on a journey of Faith, Force and Freedom."
—Pastor Matthew K. Thompson
(Senior Pastor Jubilee Christian Church), Nick's Pastor

"The year was 2008. The place was the *Visiting Room* inside MCI (Massachusetts Correctional Institution) Norfolk. The occasion was my first meeting with my new mentee, Nickolas DeJarnette. My mentorship of Nick has been pretty much constant since then. Now, 16 years later, I find myself reading and admiring his book, the one in your hands. On my first visit, I was impressed with his thoughtful demeanor and his obvious intellect. Some of the details in this book are jaw dropping, and Nick's survival, growth, and development are nothing short of a MIRACLE. If you are a lawyer, I hope it gives you insight into prison life. If you are incarcerated, I hope it gives you ideas for a way forward upon your release. If you are a mental health professional, I hope Nick's story, like the story of so many other trauma victims, renews your determination to help people like Nick. And if you are a student—in the fields of sociology, criminology, psychology, or law—this book will be one of the best educational tools of your entire education."
—The Honorable Christina Harms
(Retired Judge), Mentor of Nick

Mother:

"Nickolas, you have always been a survivor, even since you were in my womb."

Father:

"Nickolas, you are my son with the colorful robe."

In this book, I will use my life's experiences to teach the lessons I've learned throughout my life's journey regarding environment. The reader will quickly realize the importance of my mother's quote and how true such words ring regarding the first 40 years of my life. I was in my 30s when my mother shared those words with me for the first time. She began to tell me about a time in which she was pregnant with me and when my father was high on drugs and alcohol. With great detail, she explained a moment when my father violently abused her. He knocked her to the ground and began to viciously kick and stomp her. As she curled up on the floor, wrapping her arms around her pregnant stomach to protect me, she feared that a single blow to the stomach would take my very life. Explaining the details of this brutal attack, her voice began to crack as tears started to form in her eyes. She said, *"Nickolas, I could not believe what I had felt. You shifted to the opposite side of my stomach as if to hide from the blows with an innate instinct of survival. It blew my mind, and I will never forget it."* *"Nickolas,"* she said, *"you have always been a survivor, even since you were in my womb."*

This notion of an "innate instinct" of survival will be made clear—and will even be confirmed—throughout the reading of this book.

Having a spirit of survival was definitely crucial and essential regarding the first 40 years of my life; however, I look forward to living out my father's quote for the following 40 years of my life because his words to me speak to thriving and being triumphant verses merely surviving. Anyone familiar with the story of Joseph—in the Bible—knows the significance of the "colorful robe." This too will be made clear throughout the reading of this book.

CONTENTS

INTRODUCTION

My mother was a prostitute; my father was a pimp; I bet I got your attention now.

It is an absolute euphemism to say that environment played a major role in my life, both positively and negatively. When I began to understand the power and *absolute severity of environment*, I realized and said to myself, "Nick, if you change your environment, you will literally change the outcome of your life."

I invite you as the reader to go on a step-by-step journey with me from abuse and brokenness to healing and development, from homelessness and life in the "system" (*Department of Children and Family, Department of Youth Services,* and *Department of Corrections*) to *Boston University* and business ownership, and from a household and family of murderers and career criminals to strategically choosing friends and family (environment) who are supporters and encouragers. As the reader, you will learn how I went from an environment of pimps, prostitutes, drug dealers, drug users, gang bangers, thugs, career criminals, and inmates to an environment of chosen friends and family made up of pastors, college professors, entrepreneurs, celebrities, professional athletes, a former police officer and judge—individuals who genuinely care and push me to do better.

Although this step-by-step journey is filled with "R-Rated" details that may not be suitable for children, it will also illustrate a battle from alcoholism and drug addiction to sobriety and the best version of myself that I ever experienced. This journey involves the details of a life of crime and tearing communities down—and the experiences that led to the desire of being an agent for change. This book explains how I went from being raided by the first *C-PAC* unit to ever exist in *Worcester Massachusetts* (a combined intelligence task force made up of agents from the FBI, ATF, US Marshals, DEA, and State Police who collaborated with Worcester detectives and Worcester Vice Squad) to receiving a thank you letter from the commissioner of the *Boston Police Department.* From one end of the spectrum to the other, the following pages guide the reader through a metamorphosis of perspective—from being a person who hated authority and those involved with law and law enforcement to being someone who embraced having a probate court judge step into my life in my late 20's as a mother figure/ mentor. This metamorphosis of perspective also included having a multimillionaire/ former police officer as a role model, mentor, and financial coach/advisor—and, overall, going from 7 criminal charges and 7 Superior Court indictments to 7 streams of income and 7 figures in revenue all by simply choosing to change my environment and by controlling what I allowed into my life in a variety of different ways.

Nonetheless, this newfound revelation of mine regarding the *absolute severity of environment*, has been known, studied, and explained for thousands of years. Some of the greatest minds including doctors, scientists, philosophers, psychologists, sociologists, astrologists, and religious scholars (and their teachings/literature) have been revealing the power and effect of environment—and its ability to transform behavior and even biology. The mere thought that environment can actually altar biology is almost mind blowing. According to Oxford Languages, biology is defined as "the study of living organisms, divided into many specialized fields that cover their morphology, physiology, anatomy, behavior, origin, and distribution." Who would have thought that environment could be so powerful?

I cannot number the countless times— during my studies at *Boston University* in the fields of sociology, psychology, and criminology— that I came across the famous argument of "Nature vs Nurture." I, truly, thought it was a senseless argument because it is apparent to me that it is not possible for one to exist without being affected by the other. However, I am not writing in an attempt to make or break that argument; some of the greatest minds have already done so, and both sides have made compelling arguments.

Instead, I am writing about the *absolute severity of environment*, and how *simply* it can be understood—and used to revolutionize one's entire life.

Yes, it can be extremely interesting to learn how certain environments including climate (weather and temperature), for example, have actually altered the biology and physiology of humans, animals, and other species. It can also be interesting for some to learn about studies conducted on siblings, fraternal twins, and identical twins, who were raised in two completely different households—and received completely different educations and had completely different opportunities in life—and what the outcome of such studies revealed.

On the contrary, I am going to keep things extremely simple and basic. For example, if you had two roses and placed each one into its own vase containing liquid— one vase having water in it and the other vase containing gasoline—what would be the result of each rose? Very simple and basic—wouldn't you say? The vase containing water would cause the rose to live longer; whereas, the vase containing gasoline would simply expedite the death of the rose. Thus, the *absolute severity of environment.* SIMPLE RIGHT?

Before we dive into the first chapter of this book, I would like us to take a look at a few more examples that we commonly hear about, witness, or experience on a more regular basis. I will point out the example; you draw the conclusion:

* Parents who pay tens of thousands of dollars (sometimes hundreds of thousands of dollars) to place their children in private schools—ENVIRONMENT

* Students who decide to go to college but live off campus— and have friends, parents, and mentors who suggest and highly recommend that they live on campus to have the *"FULL college experience"* of campus life—ENVIRONMENT

* Criminal offenders who are released on parole and/or probation and are ordered to refrain from going back into their old neighborhoods and from associating with other "ex-offenders"—ENVIRONMENT

* Children who grow up in urban neighborhoods whose main incentive for success is to "move their mama out of the hood"—ENVIRONMENT

These are just a few examples that we encounter in life that suggest that there is an *absolute severity of environment.* My goal here is not to prove this fact; it has already been proven—by minds much greater than my own. My goal, more importantly, is to illustrate (step-by-step) how my environment played a negative role in the direction of my life—and to effectively guide every individual who reads this book into a life of prosperity (physically, mentally, emotionally, psychologically, financially, and most importantly spiritually) by simply changing your environment into a reflection of what you desire your life to look like/be.

This book is my attempt to sufficiently express the importance of the true meaning of 1 Corinthians 15:33: "bad company, corrupts good character."

Where I'm from, people often overlook or underestimate the *absolute severity of environment.*

> *"Environment is so powerful that—if it changes—whatever is within it, must also change."*
> — *Nickolas DeJarnette*

Although we see and experience this truth on a daily basis, we only seem to recognize the importance of environment when the outcome happens to be a negative one—but by that point, it is too late. For example, the ice cream melted because the freezer was not cold enough—or the milk went bad because someone left it out on the kitchen counter too long. Another popular example would be the person who got a sunburn because they stayed out in the sun longer than they should have—environment. I confess, I typically pay more attention to environment when it starts to make me feel uncomfortable—when I'm becoming *too hot* or too cold—or if I feel *closed in* or *trapped*.

However, on the flip side of things, both farmers and gardeners, for instance, not only recognize and understand the importance of environment when planting seed and nurturing agriculture—their focus is on the positive outcome of the blossom: fruit, vegetables, flower, or rearing healthy animals. In fact, their (farmers and gardeners) model is, "soil is everything." These *farmers* and *gardeners* are visionaries who strategically and diligently work the ground (soil) during a specific season in the hopes of reaping a harvest. They are the same visionaries mentioned previously who place their children in private schools and prepare them for college life. They do their best to create a positive and thriving environment for their children to grow up in. Throughout this book, I'm going to refer to these visionaries as *"Master Farmers/ Gardeners."*

Master Farmers/Gardeners know that soil is made up of minerals, organic minerals, water, and air. However, the appropriate balance of nutrients and texture is crucial regarding the richness of the soil. Therefore, both farmers and gardeners go to great lengths to understand, test, and manipulate their soil for optimal results.

Testing the soil allows one to see if their soil is out of balance. Soil can sometimes have too much acid or alkaline— or pH levels could be too high or too low. More specifically, Sulfur is used if pH levels are too high, and limestone is used if pH levels are too low. More importantly, different plants have different preferences. For instance, rhododendrons, blueberries, and azaleas do better in soil with higher acidic levels; whereas, other plants need acidic levels to be much lower. At this point, it may not be evident why the appropriate balance of nutrients and texture is so important, or how learning about rhododendrons, blueberries, and azaleas can revolutionize your entire life; none the less, it will all become evident as you turn the pages. If you are not already a *Master Farmers/Gardeners,* you will be by the end of this book. Although I do consider myself to be a *"Master Farmers/Gardeners,"* I—in no way—believe that I have *"arrived."* However, during this journey of life, I now have a proven blueprint that expedites growth and development—leaving no excuse for anyone who desires to become the best possible version of oneself.

My hope is that this book will make it into juvenile detention facilities, county jails, state prisons, and federal penitentiaries across the nation. I pray that colleges across the country—specifically in the fields of criminology, sociology, and related fields—will invite me to speak on this subject regarding *the absolute severity of environment* and even assign this book to students, so they can hear it directly *"from the horses month."*

PART: 1 THE DANGERS OF A POOR/NEGATIVE ENVIRONMENT

A BRIEF SUMMARY OF MY ENVIRONMENT

"Bad company, corrupts good character."
(1 Corinthians 15:33)

> *"… and he has two murders on his criminal record. My father's sister—Julia Miller—shot and murdered a man in Worcester Massachusetts."*

My Immediate Environment

You see, when I talk about environment, I am not necessarily talking about the state (Massachusetts) that I am from, or the city that I am from (Worcester), or even the neighborhood—the "hood" that I am from. No! When I speak about environment, I am referring to my "Immediate Environment," my household and family—those who are intimate and of close proximity. For example, I have an older brother who is 10 years older than myself—his name is Alexander DeJarnette Jr. (we call him Meat), and he has two murders on his criminal record. My father's sister—Julia Miller—shot and murdered a man in Worcester Massachusetts. My father, after (one of the many times he was) being released from either county jail or state prison, was placed on parole by the Commonwealth. The only problem with this was that they gave him a female parole officer, and my father was a pimp and had "the gift to gab." He was a very handsome and charming young man back then, and he certainly was extremely influential and witty. Before long, he started sleeping with his female parole officer, and eventually began pimping her. He would later go on to shoot a man with his parole officers gun—and her father was a judge. This information was blasted all over the news: the Commonwealth created and managed a system to keep ex-offenders in check, and this one man manipulated that system and embarrassed the Commonwealth. As a young boy, I remember hearing all of the noise: people ranting and raving about my father. I remember one time in particular, I actually saw a newspaper article with my father on the front page—and oh, how I would have loved to see a picture of my father on the front page doing something heroic and being a role model— instead, he was lying face down on the ground with multiple police officers standing over him, each with 1 foot on my father's back, shoulders back, and arms folded with big smiles—posing for a picture in the "Worcester Telegram & Gazette" newspaper. I will not even attempt to explain what that does to an 8-year-old little boy—psychologically, mentally, and emotionally.

> *"I will not even attempt to explain what that does to an 8-year-old little boy—psychologically, mentally, and emotionally. "*

My mother, on the other hand—as previously mentioned—was a prostitute. She also has been charged and arrested for a laundry list of crimes and felonies. In fact, there are rumors that my mother committed crimes that the world is unaware of, and because such crimes do not have a "Statute of Limitation," and because my mother is still alive while I am writing this book, I will not mention the crimes of such rumors. I will now move on to an older brother who is two years older than myself, Alexander DeJarnette III (the 3rd). Without getting into the long list of crimes that he has committed, I will refer to the one crime that dramatically changed the course of his life (and not for the better May I say). When he was 17 years old, he shot a man approximately 5 to 7 times in the neck, chest, and back. Fortunately, for the victim, he survived, so my brother was charged with attempted murder and sentenced to 10 to 15 years in prison when he was 17 years old.

Furthermore—and although I would love to say that this above-mentioned *Immediate Environment* left me unscarred and unscathed —unfortunately, that is not the case. My first crime was in 1988; I was eight years old, in the crime was "breaking and entering." This was my first encounter with the law/system. I would continue breaking the law and going in and out of the system throughout my entire childhood, teenage, and young adult years—going in and out of DSS (Department of Social Services) Foster homes, DYS (Department of Youth Services) juvenile lockup/detention center, and then jail (as soon as I was old enough to go at the age of 17). By the time I was 22 years old, I had earned myself a 15-to-17-year prison sentence, with 15 of those years being a "minimum mandatory" sentence—meaning that I had to serve 15 years "day for day" without the possibility of earning "good time" or being released early on parole and/or probation. After shooting a man three times in broad daylight and being caught in a drug raid, I was charged with attempted murder and drug trafficking. I was raided by seven different units including *FBI, ATF, US Marshals, DEA, State Police, Worcester Detectives* and *Worcester Vice Squad*. I would later be indicted for a half kilo of cocaine, ecstasy, amitriptyline, a few pounds of marijuana, a gun, and over 300 rounds of ammunition.

At this point, I am confident that you are beginning to understand what I mean when I refer to my environment—my *Immediate Environment*. In addition, I have a younger brother, Brandan DeJarnette—who is six years younger than myself—and a younger sister, Ashley DeJarnette—who is eight years younger than myself. Just as you can imagine—*"the apple does not fall far from the tree"*—they too have their own laundry lists of crimes and felonies which include attempted murder, multiple assault and battery charges, high speed chases, drug distribution, and more. Unfortunately, environment played a major role in the outcome of their lives as well.

CHAPTER 2

AN ENVIRONMENT OF ABUSE: The Pain, Hurt, Trauma, and PTSD of Environment

*"Plans fail for lack of counsel,
but with many advisers they succeed."*
(Proverbs 15:22)

Conception & Birth

Conceived at *MCI Walpole State Prison* in 1979, the environment of my very conception was not ideal to say the least, nor was my birthing into this world. Out of all four of my mother's children, I was recently informed that my birth/delivery was the most challenging. Feet first with the umbilical cord wrapped around my neck and armpit—the doctor had to stick both hands inside of my mother multiple times to get things right. First, he had to turn me around; then, he had to get the umbilical cord from around my neck (because it had begun to strangulate me), and then he had to untangle the cord from my armpit because it was cutting off my oxygen supply. As I reflect on the life stories of *Joyce Meyers* and *Sarah Jakes* Roberts (the devil starts early), I can't help but to believe (and hope) that God has something phenomenal in store for me. Something "exceedingly abundantly above all that [I] ask or think, according to the power that works in [me]" (Ephesians 3:20 NKJV).

> *"... the man came outside with a firearm. My father rushed towards the individual and the man began to fire his gun."*

Passenger Door Bullet Holes

I remember it like it was yesterday, 1984. The sun was out, the day was bright, and I was taking a ride with my father. We were on Chandler Street in Worcester Massachusetts, and my father pulled over to the right side of the street. He said, "wait right here; I'll be right back." He got out of the car and began to walk up to the front entrance of a building, where he began to argue with an individual. The argument did not last long before my father struck the individual and they began to fight. I watched my father beat this man up in broad daylight. As the man had gotten free from my father's grip— walking backwards up a set of stairs—he told my father to wait right here while he went upstairs to get his gun. I watched my father come back to the car, but he had no intention of leaving. He reached into the backseat and pulled out a baseball bat. As my father began to walk towards the front entrance of the building again, the man came outside with a firearm. My father rushed towards the individual and the man began to fire his gun. After several shots rang out, and several bullets struck the passenger side door of my father's car (right where I was sitting), somehow my father beat this man with the baseball bat without getting struck by a single bullet. I watched my father beat this man with the baseball bat, then walk back to the car and drive off.

One could only assume that my father was high on drugs and/or alcohol, but his temper was just as intoxicating as both, so I cannot say for sure.

We pulled up to a location on Piedmont Street in Worcester, where my mother was walking the street—prostituting herself. My father got out of the car and began to speak with my mother, when she began to scream and pound her fists on my father's chest as he tried to hold her and calm her down. She could see the bullet holes in the passenger door where I was sitting. I could hear my mother's words as she screamed, "You almost killed my baby. You almost killed my baby."

If I had to guess, I would say that I was probably 5 or 6 years old when this took place. After watching me tell this short story on a YouTube video, my mother called me to tell me that I was only 4 years old when the shooting took place. Thinking back and realizing, if I were an inch or two taller, or if I would have leaned forward or backwards, my very life would have been taken that day, at the age of 4 years old.

"Because my father was a thug and a pimp... and because our mother was a prostitute, we were left unattended and unsupervised on a regular basis."

The Development of PTSD and Claustrophobia

Because my father was a thug and a pimp who spent the majority of my life going in and out of county jails and state prisons—and because our mother was a prostitute who tried her best to keep her *professional* life away from home, we were left unattended and unsupervised on a regular basis. During those times of being left unattended and unsupervised—and well before I started experiencing the abuse of adults—I was constantly and consistently being abused by my older brother, *Alexander DeJarnette III* (The 3rd), who is two years older than myself. My older brother, Alexander DeJarnette III (who we call Al) was my mother's first child, and when I came into the picture (approximately two years later), he hated the attention I received as the *new* baby in the family. He hated it so much that as a three-year-old, he would bite my feet until I would scream out loud and cry—something that I did not learn of until I was well into my 30s. Unfortunately for me, this phase of jealousy and abuse was not a phase at all. In other words, it did not *come and go* in an expected/rational/understandable amount of time. In fact, it remained for the majority of my life and could possibly still remain today—of course, I am referring to the jealousy part (not the abuse) because I do not get close enough to him today to be abused, nor would I allow it if I did.

Sadly enough, what had started as the simple and understandable jealousy of an only child now having to deal with the loss of attention due to the birth of a sibling—had later began to metamorphous into a "Cain & Abel" like hatred that my older brother Al had and kept towards myself. Sometimes I wonder if he ever did try to kill me when I was a child/baby during a time when I was just too young to remember and speak up, or if his jealousy and hatred stayed only on the sadistic level of torture, so he could continually get "a fix" by watching my pain and discomfort.

When I was six years old, he convinced me to see if I could fit my entire body into a suitcase. Then, he zipped the suitcase up, placed it in the closet, turned the volume on the television up high, and closed the bedroom door, so no one could hear me scream. This was the start to me developing a case of claustrophobia.

One day (around the age of 5 or 6), my brother and I were playing *hide and go seek*. Right in our backyard was an old fashion, broke down, abandoned refrigerator. Now this was not one of the refrigerators that had the doors that were held shut by magnetic force; this was one of the old fashion refrigerators that had a metal latch handle that you lift up to unlock/open the refrigerator door. This refrigerator was knocked over on its side, and I—being the young clever lad that I was—thought that it would be an amazing place to hide, but I also knew that I should not allow the door to close because I would be stuck inside. So, I crawled into the refrigerator and left the door slightly cracked, with the expectation of watching my brother search for me unsuccessfully. I can image the slight grin on my face and satisfaction in my spirit— thinking that I had picked the best hiding spot in the yard. When all of a sudden, the door slammed shut, and I could hear my brother laughing and his footsteps as he ran away. Immediately overwhelmed with fear, I screamed and shouted and screamed and shouted. All I could think of is suffocating and dying. In a complete panic and crying hysterically, I continued to scream and shout scream and shout.

> *"When all of a sudden, the door slammed shut, and I could hear my brother laughing and his footsteps as he ran away."*

Hoping that someone would hear me, I continued to scream and shout and scream and shout. All types of thoughts ran through my mind. I thought my brother would leave me here as a joke and go down the street to one of his friends' houses and play all day long until I died. So I continued to scream and shout and scream and shout. As breathing became more and more difficult—whether it was from a lack of oxygen or the placebo effect of my fear—in an outrage of fear and panic, I punched and kicked the refrigerator door, screaming and shouting at the top of my lungs. I do not know how long I remained inside of that refrigerator, but I do know that it felt like an eternity. After an *eternity like* time frame of fear, panic, and hysteria, the door opened. I can hear my brother laughing and his footsteps as he ran away; as to say something along the lines of, "*Where were you Nick? You did such a good job hiding that I could not find you.*" Shortly thereafter, when I did see my brother, I had a face that was still beet red, full of tears and covered with anger and rage. And with that face, I just stared at him with a look to let him know that I had known what he had done. It was this incident along with the suitcase experience that made me severely claustrophobic.

> *"So I would bang my head up against the cement walls and rip my hair out of my own head because the claustrophobia would kick in..."*

The severity of my claustrophobia would later be exposed (approximately 10 years later) when I was *locked up* at *Westborough Secure Detention Center* (in Westborough Massachusetts) by the *Department of Youth Services* (DYS) for my first gun charge at the age of 15. I had been locked up before, but every other facility was in a large open space like a dormitory or basketball court (with bunkbeds) or a house type facility, and I knew when I would be released. However, at *Westborough Secure*, they placed us in real cells, and I had absolutely no idea when I was going home. So I would bang my head up against the cement walls and rip my hair out of my own head because the claustrophobia would kick in—being locked in a small place without knowing when I would be let out. The staff members would pull me out of the cell and restrain me in an attempt to stop me from hurting myself. At that point, I would fight back: punching, kicking, scratching, biting— doing anything I could to get them off of me. The mere fact that they were restraining me—against my own will and with limited ability of movement—increased the feeling of claustrophobia all the more.

Before I knew it, I was wrestling with several staff members— twice (maybe three or four times) my size—until I completely exhausted myself and fell asleep in their arms. Night after night, this became our *ritual*. When it became *lock down time*, the staff would come to my cell (along with a female counselor) and open the gate, and we would begin to fight. We would bring the fight into the counselor's office where the floors were carpeted and—night after night—I would fight these men, and they would restrain me until I completely exhausted myself and fell asleep in their arms. Every night the men would restrain me, and the woman's soft voice would talk me through the process. Almost as if a mother was reading a bedtime story to her child.

I do not want to get too far ahead of ourselves; I will eventually touch on my teenage years later on in this book. The purpose of me sharing this experience was to illustrate the severity of the claustrophobia that I suffered due to the actions of my older brother. However, for the sake of telling my story in chronological order, I would like the reader to return with me to the age of 6 years old.

> *"I remember a time when my mother ran away from my father when he was incarcerated and she took us to the opposite side of the country, California."*

Wet Shorts on A Slide

Just recently— and at the age of 41–I showed my wife a large scar shaped like the moon on the bottom of my foot. I then began to tell her where the scar came from. I remember a time when my mother ran away from my father when he was incarcerated and she took us to the opposite side of the country, California. I remember being left with my older brother Al at a local outdoor swimming pool. After having my fun in the water, I decided to go to the playground that was on the opposite side of the fence. While unattended and unsupervised, I left the community pool area and walked over to the playground. While playing in this unoccupied playground, I continued to climb the ladder of the slide, and slide down it as fast as I could. I quickly noticed that having wet shorts and no shoes made the slide experience much faster and more appealing. Each attempt, I would try to go faster than the one before. Over and over again, I would climb the ladder and then thrust myself down the slide. One thing I was very good at as a child was being able to create my own fun. I had absolutely no problem at all being by myself. In fact, most times it was the safest time of my life. Al, on the other hand, did not like to be alone, and he certainly did not like how easy it was for me to have so much fun without him. So his 8 year old mind decided that he was going to put an end to my having fun without him. And with the creative mind that he has always had, he figured out exactly how he was going to succeed. After watching me countless times go up and down the slide, he found the perfect red brick and a nice big round piece of glass. Then, very quickly and without my knowledge, while I was climbing up the ladder to get to the top of the slide, he placed the brick exactly where my feet would hit the ground when I would come to the bottom of the slide. He then placed a very large, curved piece of broken glass on top of the brick with the sharp edges facing up. Standing at the top of the slide, I was filled with ambition, filled with energy, and filled with the desire to go down that slide faster than I had ever gone down it before. So with all of my strength, I thrusted myself down the slide as fast as I could, and with all that speed and all that momentum, my feet hit the ground with such force—one foot hitting the ground and the other foot stepping perfectly onto the glass that was intentionally leveraged by the brick. Of course, I screamed out loud. I dropped to the ground in pain—having absolutely no idea what had just happened to me. Looking down at my foot and seeing more blood than I had ever seen before in my entire life, who comes along to help pick me up and walk me down the street (towards the pool we were left at), but my brother Al. An ambulance was called, I was rushed to the hospital, and the doctor took the large piece of glass out of my foot and stitched me up. My brother looked like the responsible hero, and nobody ever knew what actually happened to me that day.

> *"Looking down at my foot and seeing more blood than I had ever seen before in my entire life..."*

Overall, our time in California was short-lived. When my father got out of prison, he found my mother and us, and took us back to Worcester Massachusetts. No one knew how he got out so fast, or how he even found us. But what they did know about my father was that he was connected and very influential.

Home Sweet Home

At this same tender age of six, I watched my father argue with my mother about taking us out of the state and letting another man put his hands on us. It was a man name Joey who took us out to California; he was referred to as my mother's boyfriend, but in hindsight, he was most likely her pimp for a very short period of time. Now that we were back home, the chaos continued as usual, and Bonnie and Clyde— I mean my mother and father—continued with their life of crime, violence, guns, drugs, alcohol, pimping, and prostitution. One evening, while playing Atari with Al, our father gave us a 40 ounce of malt liquor to drink between the two of us. That was my first experience with alcohol, but it certainly was not my last.

Home for us at the time was an apartment in a three-unit house on 57 Coral Street in Worcester Massachusetts. That house burned down in 1987, and we ended up in a homeless shelter. After some time in the homeless shelter, my mother eventually received some assistance from the government and was able to get us a new apartment on 8 Ashmont Avenue in Worcester Massachusetts.

New Home, New Problems

If you thought things were bad for me at the age of six, by the time I turned eight, things had only gotten worse. For some reason, human nature leads us to believe that things will be better in a new place, and for some; however, it actually is. Unfortunately for myself, this was not the case. We had moved to a very racist area in a time (the 1980s) where interracial couples and children were not only almost non-existent, they were also not welcomed or tolerated. It was at this beautiful and somewhat innocent age (8) that I first experienced racism amongst a bunch of other challenges that would dramatically effect, alter, define, blemish, hinder, wound, scar, and cripple my childhood, teenage years, and early adulthood. Such challenges/experiences affected me physically, mentally, emotionally, psychologically, financially, educationally, occupationally, and even spiritually.

> *"In regards to the racism, I did not know that I was experiencing racism at the time; I had only known that I was experiencing pain and discomfort."*

In regard to the racism, I did not know that I was experiencing racism at the time; I had only known that I was experiencing pain and discomfort. What I mean by this is that I had a third grade teacher who was racist; her name was Mrs. Oliver. And to be completely honest, I did not even know what racism was at that age; however, when I was in Mrs. Oliver's class, she would randomly squeeze and twist my arm, and I had absolutely no idea why she was doing this to me. Furthermore, although all of my papers were graded in the high 90s and 100s, my report cards would display C's and D's. There was two major problems with this dilemma because being in a home full of drugs, alcohol, violence, and abuse—going to school was my refuge and place of peace and fun. I remember hating when school got out. I would see other kids so happy when the school bell rang, and the school day was over. I would see them running to their parents vehicles or running to the school buses—happy to be getting out of school. I on the other hand, hated it. I was scared, nervous, with butterflies in my stomach every day, having no idea what I was going home to. So not only was I physically being abused by my teacher, but I had now lost my place of peace and fun—simply leaving one place of abuse (home) only to go to another place of abuse (school). As a result, this not only left me confused but also scared and then angry.

> *"But my mother did not stop there—with the only biracial children in the entire school, my mother went straight to the NAACP as a white woman with colored children."*

Not to mention, I took pride in my schoolwork—I focused and worked hard to obtain high scores on each assignment. It gave me some feeling of value and self-worth. Moreover, I did not want the poor grades reflected on my report cards to be another excuse for my father to beat me. I valued my work so much that I hung up all my assignments on my bedroom wall. The good thing about that was that I had actually kept all of the evidence that would prove that my grades should be higher. My mother in turn went up to the school complaining, but the school refused to make any changes because doing so would simply be proving/admitting that one of their own was doing something wrong in the first place. But my mother did not stop there—with the only biracial children in the entire school, my mother went straight to the NAACP as a white woman with colored children. As soon as the NAACP got involved, the entire school administration sang a different song. I was immediately, and I mean immediately (the following day), placed into a different classroom on a completely different floor/level of the school (so I never had to see that woman's face again), and by the next report card term, my grades displayed all A's. Yes, my brother Al and I were the only biracial kids in the entire school, but there was three other colored kids, and they were brothers: Johnny, Jackie, and Jeremiah. They were my best friends, and they were Panamanian.

"I could hear my mother screaming at the top of her lungs as my father brutally and viciously beat her for—what seemed to be countless hours."

Kitchen Nightmare

It is now 1988, and I was eight years old. I could hear my mother screaming at the top of her lungs as my father brutally and viciously beat her for—what seemed to be countless hours. We lived on the second floor in a three decker (3 unit) house (on 8 Ashmont Avenue in Worcester Massachusetts). Our first-floor neighbor was a racist white man who was approximately 400 pounds and had two very big German Shepherd dogs. When my father would be away in jail or prison, he (the 400 pound neighbor) would make disrespectful and racist comments to my mother—calling her a "Nigger Lover" among other things. Our third-floor neighbors were a Jewish couple who had a son who was around my age. I mention these neighbors because they would never intervene, try to help, or at least call the police—when my father was brutally beating my mother. I know they could hear what was going on because the walls were "paper-thin," and I could hear whenever the boy on the third floor was running around upstairs. Furthermore, when my siblings and I would be running around making noise— and when my father was away in jail or prison—the first-floor neighbor would bang on his ceiling in an attempt to get us to quiet down.

Along with the sound of my mother screaming and crying—and begging my father to stop—was also the sound of furniture being thrown and knocked over.

"There was blood everywhere—blood on the walls, blood on the floor, blood all over the kitchen cabinets and table..."

We, Al being 10 years old, Brandan being almost 3 at the time, and myself, we're all in our bedroom with the door closed. Al was sitting on his twin bed, and I was sitting on my twin bed with Brandan. The noise continued and the screaming got worse—as if my mother was scared for her life. I remember Brandan jumping out of the bed and running straight towards the bedroom door. He stopped right in front of the door, clinched his whole body, and began to scream. His body completely stiff, standing on the tip of his toes, with his arms by his side squeezing his fists—he screamed. I immediately jumped out of the bed, ran up to him from behind, wrapped my hand around his mouth, picked him up, and brought him back into the bed with me. I was afraid that my father would hear him and come into the room to start beating on us. Eventually, things got quiet, and we would all finally fall asleep. The next morning, I opened our bedroom door (our bedroom was right next to the kitchen)— and gripped with fear— I saw what looked like a murder scene in a movie. There was blood everywhere—blood on the walls, blood on the floor, blood all over the kitchen cabinets and table—and my first thought/wonder was if my mother was still alive. My father came out of their bedroom and instructed Al and I to clean up the mess. And there I was—8 years old with my 10-year-old brother by my side—on my hands and knees, cleaning up my own mothers blood. (Despite the many years of counseling as a child with Dr. Fisher and Shirley Williams at the Worcester Youth Guidance Center—along with the many years of work that I put into my own healing and deliverance with God and other professionals—it is still hard recalling some of my childhood experiences.) When the moment arrived and my mother finally came out of their bedroom, I could not believe what I saw. My mother did not look like my mother at all. In fact, her face did not even look human. Her face was swollen, her eyes were the size of pool balls, the white in her eyeballs were filled with blood, her jaw was broken, her entire face was black and blue with blood and mascara all mixed together. My mother did not look like my mother at all.

Over the course of my parents' 16-year marriage, my father broke both of my mother's arms, both of her legs, and several of her ribs. He broke her jaw, he once put her face through a wall, and he once hung her out of a three-story building.

> *"...my father asked me if it was true that I had tried to stab my brother Al with a steak knife. I said yes..."*

Bumper Beatin

My father got wind that I had tried to stab my brother Al, when I was 12 years old, and he (Al) was fourteen. At this time, my father was incarcerated at the "Boston Pre-Release Center," so he was able to leave the prison for certain periods of time. While visiting the house of a church pastor, my father told me to come outside and take a walk with him— my mother, Al, Brandan, and Ashley stayed inside. As we walked down the street, my father asked me if it was true that I had tried to stab my brother Al with a steak knife. I said yes, and begin to explain to him why. As we continued to walk, my father found and picked up a pretty good size piece of wood. He walked me to my mother's car and began to give me instructions. He said, "Nickolas I want you to place your hands on the front bumper of the car. If you take your hands off of the bumper, your beatin is going to start all over again." I placed my hands on the bumper of the car as my father raised the wood in his hand. He came down with the wood, crushing my back. "CRACK"—the sound was loud, and the pain was unbearable—and my hands immediately came off the bumper. I looked at my father, and he looked at me—and said, "Son, don't let this keep happening." Then, with pain in my back and tears in my eyes—body trembling—I leaned over and grabbed that bumper as tight as I possibly could while my father raised the wood that was in his hand for a second time. "CRACK"—the sound was loud, and the pain was unbearable—but my hands did not come off of the bumper. I looked at my father, and he looked at me. With pain in my back and tears in my eyes—body trembling—I continued to hold that bumper as tight as I possibly could while my father raised the wood that was in his hand for the third time. "CRACK"—the sound was loud, and the pain was unbearable—but my hands did not come off of the bumper. At this point, an African American woman across the street came out of her house— screaming with a load voice, "You better leave that boy alone. You better leave that boy alone before I call the cops." I looked at my father, and he looked at me. With pain in my back and tears in my eyes—body trembling—I continued to hold that bumper as tight as I possibly could while my father raised the wood that was in his hand for the fourth time. "CRACK"—the sound was loud, and the pain was unbearable—but my hands did not come off of the bumper. I looked at my father with tears in my eyes, and he looked at me. "CRACK."

"CRACK,"

"CRACK,"

"CRACK,"

"CRACK,"

"CRACK,"

After a beating that felt like it would never end, it eventually did. From the back of my shoulders to the back of my knees, my flesh was torn, swollen, welted, bruised, and bleeding. Then, my father made me sit in the car—adding pressure to the wounds. He made me sit on what he had just done to me. Looking back on the situation now, it makes me wonder if his intention for making me sit in the car was to deliberately add to the pain, or if it was simply because he did not want to bring me back into the pastor's house in that condition. Either way, I can confidently say that sitting in the car added to the damage done physically, mentally, and emotionally.

"CRACK"—the sound was loud, and the pain was unbearable—but my hands did not come off of the bumper."

Not before long, my father came back to the car and told me to step out of the vehicle. My first thoughts were that my father was going to apologize because that is something that he would do often after beating us or physically abusing my mother. He would give us one of his famous lines—a line that I am sure many who have grown up experiencing physical discipline has heard before—"that beatin hurt me more than it hurt you." In the back of my mind, I always said, "I highly doubt it."

But no, it was not my father's desire to apologize. Instead, he said to me, "Son, I want you to know something. I want you to know that I did not stop beating you because that woman told me to stop beating you; I stopped beating you because the wood broke. Now, get back into the car." So I got back into the car and sat there by myself—sitting on what he had just done to me.

We would later drop him back off to jail—the "pre-release center"—and head home on an hour drive back to Worcester. On the way home, we stopped at a gas station, and I told my mother that I had to go pee. I went into the gas station bathroom, and seeing a mirror, I took off my shirt to look at my back. And I made a promise to myself—NEVER AGAIN!!!

CHAPTER 3

THE INFLUENCE OF ENVIRONMENT AND THE LESSONS TAUGHT

*"Train up a child
in the way he should go,
And when he is old
he will not depart from it."*
(Proverbs 22:6)

PTSD

"a psychological reaction occurring after experiencing a highly stressing event (such as wartime combat, physical violence, or a natural disaster) that is usually characterized by depression, anxiety, flashbacks, recurrent nightmares, and avoidance of reminders of the event" is how the Merriam-Webster Dictionary defines post-traumatic stress disorder (PTSD).

Direct and Indirect Influence

Not only was this "toxic and destructive environment" painful—hurting me physically, mentally, and emotionally—but it also had a major influence on me both indirectly and directly. Indirectly, I was being influenced by my father's temper and his anger issues, the verbal explosions that I witnessed, and the violence/abuse that I both witnessed and experienced. In other words, I was being trained, indirectly, how to deal with conflict and disagreements. Without taking a single note, I was learning the art of communication—volume, voice fluctuation, body language, facial expressions, mannerisms—how to yell, swear, and break things, etc. I had a front row seat—learning in the class of bad behavior without it being a requirement or chosen elective.

When other eight-year-old kids were trying on their baseball gloves for the first time and learning how to play catch with their fathers, I was being taught (directly) how to "buss a motha-fucka's head wide open with a brick." My father was teaching *Al* and I how to fight at this age, and losing was not an option. "You punch, kick, scratch, bite, stab— if there is more than one of them, you pick up a rock and hit the biggest motha-fucka first; you beat him so bad that everyone in the neighborhood will be talking about you."

When *Al* was 10 years old and I was eight, we were at Crompton Park playing with our friends. I was playing basketball—*Al* was never athletic, so he was somewhere else in the park. Long story short, a

14-year-old boy punched him in the mouth and busted his lip. I was playing basketball, so I did not see it when it happened. When the streetlights came on, we went home. When my father saw my brother's bloody lip—and when my brother told my father what had happened—my father beat us both, and then he sent us back outside with a hammer to find the kid who punched my brother. My father told us that we could not come home unless there was blood on the hammer. I would have preferred the baseball glove and a game of catch.

> *"The rap lyrics spoke about being tough and never letting anyone hurt you or disrespect you..."*

Influenced/Taught by Music, Movies, and The Streets

However, because my father spent most of my childhood going in and out of county jails and state prisons—and because my mother was never around much—I was left to being taught by other influential monsters such as music, movies, and the "streets." That day, after holding onto the bumper as if my life depended on it, and being beatin until the wood broke, I went into my bedroom, closed the door, and put on my headphones to listen to rap music. This was something that I did often; whenever I would feel alone and/or overwhelmed, stressed out and/or depressed, broken and/or hopeless. I would put on my headphones and block everything out. Little did I know, this rap music that I was using for a "getaway," using as a refuge, using for comfort and medicine was actually a cancer that was poisoning my mentality and warping my way of thinking. The rap lyrics spoke about being tough and never letting anyone hurt you or disrespect you; it's spoke about being willing to fight, stab, and shoot at any given moment. And the thought of running, retreating, or avoiding conflict all together meant that you were weak, a coward, a pussy. It spoke about making people respect you and fear you. Unfortunately, and without my knowing, this music fed my anger; it fed my bitterness, and it fed my frustration. But somehow, it seemed to be the answer to my confusion and pain. It (the rap music) gave its own definition of "manhood" which was sleeping with random/multiple women, smoking weed (marijuana), drinking alcohol, selling drugs, having lots of money, jewelry, cars, etc.

> *"And to make matters worse, everything that I was hearing in the music was what I grew up witnessing in my household and family…"*

And to make matters worse, everything that I was hearing in the music was what I grew up witnessing in my household and family—and when I stepped out of my doors and into my community, there it was again. It was not just in my "hood" (neighborhood), but it was in hoods all across America, and then all across the world. It was not just a lifestyle but a culture. There was an attitude and dress code that went with it. And almost everyone who displayed this same attitude and dress code had embraced the culture. Today they wear skinny jeans, but back then it was baggy jeans—baggy jeans that sagged below the buttocks. And it was not just here in America, but it was all across the world— kids in Russia and China were wearing baggy jeans, sagging them below their buttocks, and embracing the same rap/hip-hop culture.

In addition, if the indirect and direct influence of this rap/hip-hop culture was not toxic enough, I had become obsessed with mafia/ gangster movies— and their characters. Movies like *"The God Father,"* *"Scarface," "New Jack City," "Carlito's Way," "The Untouchables,"* *"Good Fellas," "Casino," "American Gangster," "Menace 2 Society,"* and *"Boys In The Hood"* are just a few of the movies that influenced my life, thinking, and behavior. I went from mimicking the characters to becoming them so to speak. I was 15 years old when I took over my entire projects with my marijuana operation. Living in Boston now— and seeing how small their projects are—this just sounds small and insignificant. However, my projects—*Great Brook Valley Projects*—was the largest projects in Massachusetts, and the most dangerous/deadly as well. Our projects was so big that some people wouldn't leave it for years because they didn't need to. We had our own hospital in the projects, two grocery stores, multiple daycare centers, a softball field, several basketball courts and handball courts, a swimming pool, etc. (did I mention a hospital and two grocery stores). Again, I was 15 years old when I took over my entire projects with my marijuana operation. I had men twice my age working for me and men twice my age who wanted me dead. My marijuana operation brought in more than the cocaine, crack-cocaine, and heroin drug spots combined. They called me "Nick with the Nics" because I sold "nickel-bags" ($5.00 bags of Marijuana). Back then, I would bag up $2,200 of "nickel-bags" from a single pound of weed—and sold approximately 1.5 pounds a day for years. I knew I was making a lot of money, but because I spent money recklessly and took care of a lot of people, I never really knew "*how much*" I was making. As fast as it came was as fast as it left. Today, being the owner of multiple companies and understanding the importance of numbers (profit & loss), I now realize that as a 15-year-old kid, I was bring in approximately $1.2 million annually off of my "nickel-bag" operation alone. This did not include the sales in which I sold weight (bulk—ounces and pounds in a single transaction), nor did it include the cocaine, crack-cocaine, ecstasy, or acid (LSD) that I sold as well. No wonder I had thugs twice my age trying to rob me.

> *"One of Johnny's men approached me and told me that I better close down my operation. I laughed at him and said, 'Johnny who.'"*

I remember my first real mafia move— thinking strategically and approaching my competition regarding business. I had gotten locked up at the age of 15 for my first gun and crack-cocaine charge. When I had gotten out, there was a new boss in town, Johnny, and I had to start from the bottom—from scratch. This dude was a muscle head— Puerto Rican dude who had his hand in everything. Not only did he have the largest marijuana spot in my projects (only because I was gone may I add), but he also was moving cocaine, crack-cocaine, heroin, and guns—and had men all over the projects working for him. My father instilled in me a "bow to no man" type of attitude, so I walked freely in my projects as I started up my marijuana operation again—even selling on Johnny's block. One of Johnny's men approached me and told me that I better close down my operation. I laughed at him and said, "Johnny who." Not out of disrespect, I really did not know who Johnny was; I had just been released from a juvenile detention facility. In addition, that was just how I moved— more focused on what I was trying to accomplish and caring very little about the next man or his opinion. So, there I was about 165 lbs. max—17 years old—telling one of Johnny's men (who was most likely in his 30s), "Johnny who?" Another one of Johnny's men was there smoking a cigarette and leaning up against a car he was speaking Spanish and telling the other man to slap me and to take whatever was in my pockets. Although Johnny did not know who I was, these men did, and they knew I had a reputation for carrying guns and being willing to shoot in broad daylight. As I walked away, a little young homie from around the way (also Puerto Rican) asked me if I knew what the guy was saying because he was speaking Spanish. I told him no, but I understood completely what was being said. The young Homie said, "I can't believe you said that; you said, 'Johnny who' and the other guy was telling him to slap you and empty your pockets, but he just stood there and did nothing while you walked away— I can't believe it."

I knew I had to do something; there was a marijuana drought not just in Worcester but all over the *state*. I specifically went to Johnny's marijuana block because that's where all of the customers would go when they were looking for marijuana, but Johnny's men would turn them away because they had run out of "weed" (marijuana). I knew this was my opportunity to get back on top with my marijuana operation; no one could find marijuana throughout the state, and I had stumbled across the perfect "connect" (supplier)— A Jamaican dude from New York named Lucky. With plans only to succeed, I knew Johnny and his men could become problematic—and having shoot-outs over turf could end badly with me ending up either dead or in jail—totally opposite of my plans for "success." So I said to myself, "I have to get to Johny without his men being present."

He said, "what's up little hommie." I said, "I have a business proposition for you." He said, "I'm listening,"

One day, Johnny was outside of his spot with his wife; they had finished talking and she jumped into one of his trucks and drove away —and there Johnny was all alone—this was my perfect opportunity. I walked up to Johnny and said, "hey John." He said, "what's up Little Hommie." I said, "I have a business proposition for you." He said, "I'm listening," with a smirk on his face. I said, *"right now, you are losing lots of business because you don't have any weed and eventually people are going to stop coming here because they are going to believe that you are out of business. If you let me sell my weed here at your spot, the customers will be temporarily satisfied, and they will keep coming because they are getting the weed that they want. In addition, my weed is not as good as your weed; you have the best weed in the city, so when you get your weed pumping again, I will leave, and the customers will go back to you because your weed is better. We both know, if you do not sell any weed for a long period of time this spot is going to die, and you will have to start from scratch all over again."* Smoking his cigarette, he took a moment and said, *"you're smart Lil Hommie. I respect your hustle. OK, I'll let you sell here at my spot, but once I start pumping again, you have to leave. I am not saying that you have to stop selling weed, but you can't sell it around here. I'm not worried about you taking my customers because like you said I have the best weed in the city."*

BOOM, at that moment, I had completed my first strategic mafia move. Johnny ordered all his men to leave me alone while I sold marijuana at *his* spot. His men looked at me furiously as I smiled—wondering how I did it, but having no choice but to respect my game and hustle. What Johnny didn't know is that I had the best marijuana in the city, and I was not going to let any of his customers forget that. When Johnny started pumping his marijuana about a month later, I honored my word, and I left— and all of his customers came with me.

Because of the abuse that I suffered at home and because of the environments that I was consistently placed in, I was extremely cautious and well aware of my environment. As a child, I was extremely observant. Paying attention became an innate part of my being—not second nature but first nature—a *Spirit* of discernment. I had learned very young that a wise man learns from his mistakes, but an even wiser man learns from the next man's mistakes. So, I watched closely.

10 Year Drug Run

In fact, during my 10-year drug run, I had never been arrested, or charged for drug distribution. Yes, when I was 15 years old—and picked up my first gun possession charge—I had some crack-cocaine in my back pocket and claimed that it was for personal use, so I was not charged with drug distribution. And when I was 22 years old and got raided by Worcester's first C-PAC unit, it was because I had shot a man 3 times in broad daylight, and a confidential informant informed the C-PAC unit of my whereabouts. So those law enforcement officials got lucky and simply stumbled upon the drugs and other paraphernalia. So, yes, from the age of 12 to the age of 22, I outsmarted authorities regarding the distribution of narcotics. (SIDE NOTE: you may be able to outsmart man, but you will NEVER outsmart GOD!)

> *"So, yes, from the age of 12 to the age of 22, I outsmarted authorities regarding the distribution of narcotics. "*

Moreover, it was not just the amazing head on my shoulders that kept me from getting caught all those years. You see, we had a cousin who was a police officer. In fact, I did not even know that I had a cousin who was a police officer until I was a grown man and had completely left my life of crime. The reason for this was because this cousin of mine did not want anything to do with the DeJarnette family or our reputation. He did, however, always stay in touch with my *Gramma Nettie*. And every now and then, he would pay Gramma a visit and say something along the lines of, "I hear that Brenda and the kids are not doing to well." It was a no-brainer to my *Gramma*; *Big Mama* (Gramma) was a G (gangster), and she knew if my cousin (who was a police officer) was hearing something about Brenda and her kids (most likely from other police officers), it was because we were involved in something serious that needed to stop immediately. Grandma would call my mother and say, "whatever you are doing, you need to stop it right now." My mother, intern, would tell me—and we would shut things down immediately. My mama was a G too, so when she gave me that look, I knew it was time to shut things down immediately. So we would shut things down for a couple of weeks and keep our eyes and ears on the streets. I say we because (remember, at the age of 15, I was living with my mother) both my mother and my younger brother sold drugs for me as well.

Eventually, sometime during our "shut down" period, a massive drug raid would sweep our entire projects all in one night. Swat teams combined with multiple different law enforcement agencies would do multiple drug raids in the middle of the night. Everybody would be looking out of their project windows—hundreds would be flushing whatever drugs they had in the apartment down the toilet— and we would just sit at the windows, confidently and peacefully, watching multiple drug spots get raided.

> *"I, on the flipside, would wait no longer than a week for the dust to clear —before I would set up shop again— taking full advantage of the fact that all of my competition was behind bars."*

This happened at least twice during my 10-year drug run—where I would get word from mama to shut down because she got word from gramma—who got word from our cousin (the police officer). We wouldn't see another raid like that for a few years because the authorities got most of the "Big Dawgs" off the streets and confiscated excessive amounts of drugs and firearms. All parties (authority officials) were extremely busy celebrating, doing news interviews, receiving promotions, and doing their very best in court proceedings to make all of their charges stick. I, on the flipside, would wait no longer than a week for the dust to clear—before I would set up shop again— taking full advantage of the fact that all of my competition was behind bars. Overall, my hope— in sharing all of these intimate details about my life—is to paint a clear picture of all the different elements of my environment that had a major impact on the previous direction of my life, and how my environment affected me physically, mentally, emotionally, psychologically, and spiritually —while the elements of my environment influenced (both indirectly and directly) me, my development, behavior, philosophies and perspective.

"Life had spoken up so loudly and so clearly at the age of 21 that I had almost turned my life around and changed for the better—ALMOST."

Life's Lesson

Life had spoken up so loudly and so clearly at the age of 21 that I had almost turned my life around and changed for the better—*ALMOST.* You see there was a particular individual, whose name is not important, who was known for selling guns and drugs throughout the city. I will refer to this individual as Elroy (inside joke for those I grew up with) for the sake of this short story. Elroy and I crossed paths a couple of times. Late one night while sitting in my car and waiting for a friend to come out of his project building, I saw a young man running for his life and right behind him were three goons chasing him. A few nights later I was at a private party and heard the young man who was being chased that night telling the story. I said, "wow that was you, I never seen anyone run so fast," and we all started to laugh. This kid was a good kid. He was not into the street life, or the gang life, nor was he trying to be a tough guy. I found out that he was actually very good friends with a few guys who I called *brothers*—guys I grew up with. So, I asked him, "who were the guys who were chasing you, and why were they chasing you? He then explained that it was Elroy and his goons who were chasing him that night because Elroy found out that he had slept with Elroy's girlfriend. In short, I told the kid to come with me and show me where Elroy lived, so he did. When we arrived at the project building, I went to the front door and banged on it loudly. Elroy—and a couple of his goons—looked out the window. I told Elroy that if I ever found out that he or anyone he knew messed with this kid again, they were going to have problems that they would regret. Elroy knew who I was, and he agreed to leave the kid alone, so we hopped back in my car and went back to the party. The kid was shocked and extremely grateful and from that day forward, he never had a problem with Elroy and his goons ever again.

Unfortunately, that was not the last time that I would see Elroy be-cause—coincidentally and later in life—Elroy started sleeping with the female who used to braid my hair. One day, while I was over her place getting my hair braided, Elroy came over with a couple of his goons. Elroy had also made friends with a few of her cousins who were also dudes from the streets— and they too were hanging out at her place. Typical "*hood*" scenario—a bunch of people hanging out, music blast-ing, people smoking, drinking, eating, and laughing, while I was there getting my hair braided.

"Simply put, a banged him out in front of everyone and did so pretty bad."

One of my brothers happened to be with me, and for whatever reason, Elroy thought it smart to say something disrespectful to my brother. Simply put, a banged him out in front of everyone and did so pretty bad. There were rumors that Elroy came back in an SUV looking for me with some friends— friends that not only knew who I was but were also related to me (cousins of mine). When they found out that Elroy wanted to retaliate against me, they told him that in doing so— he would have serious problems with them as well. With Elroy feeling like he had no other options regarding retaliation, he decided to call the cops. And before I knew it, I was back in jail again. "No big deal," was my initial thought. I'll just bail myself out of jail and pay an attorney who will split the money with a dirty *DA* (or prosecutor), and the case will get swept under the rug. The only problem with this idea was that the courts decided to hold me without bail for 90 days this time around, and my youngest son was due to be born in a few months.

The fear and anxiety of missing my son's birth completely overtook me. I began to pray, read my Bible, pray and read some more. I spent 90 days, drawing closer to God, and begging Him to have mercy on me, so that I would not miss the birth of my son Niko. And, by the grace of God, I got out five days before Niko was born.

OK, you may be thinking, so what was the life lesson you learned? Well, after watching my son's birth, and thinking about how I had almost missed it due to smashing Elroy, I decided to give up the street life and enroll into the Navy. You see, at that point, I had only had a reckless juvenile record because I was only 21 years old and had beaten the few adult cases that I had acquired since the age of 17. So, I did not have an adult criminal record at the time. Furthermore, I had amazing referrals because a close friend of mine was in the military, so he gave me a referral and my mother-in-law was married to a Navy Seal, so I had her referral and the referral of her husband.

However, I was told by the recruiter that I was denied due to medical reasons because I have two 6-inch screws in my left ankle. However, the screws did not affect me at all. I could play sports, fight, and do anything that any other athletic man could do. In fact, I could not even feel that the screws were in my ankle in the first place. This same recruiter later told me that I should not have put my wife and children on the paperwork until after completing *Boot Camp* and being accepted. He said the true reason for my denial was that the Navy was more interested in young men fresh out of high school and college who had no dependents because financially they would be taking on that burden. Regardless of the actual reason, and/or what I was told, the truth is, I was denied, so I went back to doing the only thing that I was good at— selling drugs.

"Regardless of the actual reason, and/or what I was told, the truth is, I was denied, so I went back to doing the only thing that I was good at— selling drugs."

I would like to take a moment to pause right now, and reflect on that last sentence, and the perspective behind it. This was my mentality as a 21-year-old young man; however, I am writing this book at the age of 43 today. Currently understanding that I had my whole life ahead of me—knowing today that I did not get my degree until the age of 36. You see, my thinking/reasoning was a result of my environment. I could not think *BIGGER* because I had never seen *BIGGER*. I had heard of bigger, but bigger was for *"other people,"* and I knew this because I had never actually seen bigger in person. In addition, I had also known that I did not even have a high school diploma at that time. In fact, I had only had a GED that I had obtained at the age of 19 because it was necessary to get a job back in 1999 in Worcester Massachusetts— never studied, took the GED test while drunk, and passed with flying colors.

(Never having any intentions of furthering my education, I received my GED for the purpose of getting a job because my grandmother had told me in order to live in her house, I had to have a job. I was living with my grandmother at the time because I had recently gotten out of jail, again, at the age of 19.)

So, I was 21 years old when the Navy turned me down, and armed with only a GED, I was convinced that I would never be able to find a job that would be able to take care of myself, Crystal (the woman who I was married to at the time), and our three sons— and I was right. Where I was wrong was to think that there were no other options. Today I realize that there were actually many options, and if I had stayed faithful to God, worked hard, maybe applied for some grants and financial aid to go to a community college at night while working a job by day, I could have fought my way into a productive life for myself and family. Instead, believing what I believed, I turned my back on my walk with God for money—and told Him—He would have to understand because I was doing it for my wife and children.

After diving headfirst back into the drug game, my first purchase—like any other time I decided to sell drugs—was a gun. My plans were always to do things big, and with big money in my hood, you had to be strapped.

"After diving headfirst back into the drug game, my first purchase—like any other time I decided to sell drugs—was a gun."

However, it was still obvious to me that I had to change my perspective and even philosophies in order to be successful in the drug game. I had to minimize the risk of losing my family and freedom. You see, I was so reckless as a youth, I was willing to shoot someone over $5.00—just for GP (general principal). If they owed me the money, and did not pay, they had to be dealt with because that is what I was taught from the rap music, mafia movies and streets. So, I changed my entire perspective regarding "beef" (declaring war, smoke). I matured. I started to realize that I had too much to lose, and I told myself if I keep wiling out over five dollars, I would lose my freedom and be separated from my wife and kids—along with the fact that I would be losing large profit while incarcerated. I could only imagine how much money I lost in the 90 days that I was held because my bail was revoked for smashing Elroy.

So yes, I changed my entire perspective regarding beef. I took on a new philosophy which involved giving every worker a specific pep talk. *"I am fronting you this product; you have an option: you can pay me back or you can rip me off. If you rip me off, I will not come look for you, and there will be absolutely no consequences for your actions* (I knew that nobody actually believed that part of the spiel, but I said it and actually meant it). *However, what I am giving you is like a grain of sand on a beach compared to what I actually have, so you can rip me off and feed yourself once, or you could be loyal and feed yourself for a lifetime."* That was my spiel. I was good with math and never gave out or fronted an amount of product that could hurt me if it were lost or stolen.

(This new philosophy allowed me to scale to much higher heights in the drug game. Nevertheless, this philosophy also came from a mafia movie: The Bronx Tale—when C was chasing a guy that owed him $20, Sonny told C that he (C) *"got off easy"* because it only cost him $20 to get rid of a guy that he didn't like anyways. He told C, now that the guy owes C money, he won't come around anymore, and he certainly won't ask to borrow money again. So, overall, it cost him $20 to get rid of a problem. Money well spent.)

CHAPTER 4

THE CONSEQUENCES OF ENVIRONMENT

"For lack of guidance a nation falls,
but victory is won through many advisers."
(Proverbs 11:14)

From Vegas To Handcuffs

I knew that the type of money I wanted to make would provoke jealousy and create enemies—like it had always done—so this time around, I moved discreetly and kept a low profile. Before long, I had scaled higher than I had ever scaled before in my entire 10-year drug run. I thought I was invisible, and to a certain extent I was.

That is, until I got a phone call from Ashley—my 14-year-old little sister. She was crying and told me that my mother's boyfriend had sexually molested her. At the time, I was recording music in *Las Vegas*, and was only back home in Worcester Massachusetts to get custody of my younger brother, Brandan, who was 17 years old at the time.

(Brandan had finished his juvenile sentence, but the Department of Youth Services would not release him because he did not have a home to go to. The reason for this was because my mother was deemed to be an "Unfit Parent" by the courts and Department of Social Services. My mother called me crying, feeling guilty because she was the reason why they would not release him from the juvenile detention center, so I flew home from Vegas, filed motions in the court, and got my brother out of the "lock up facility" all in the same day. I then took him home to live with myself, crystal, and our three sons.)

After receiving the phone call from Ashley, I grabbed a hammer, jumped in my car, and sped over to my mother's apartment building. The whole drive over, I was thinking about crystal and our children. I had taken on the belief that the music that I was recording in Vegas was my chance to get out of the street life. In my mind, I had finally made it. I was recording music for a record label at the original *Digital Studios* in Las Vegas, Nevada. I was hanging out with different celebrities and even recorded music on the same microphone as some of the biggest names in the music industry— *DMX, Sean Diddy Combs, Garth Brooks, Dream*, etc. Although everything inside of me just wanted to put a bullet in the head of my mother's boyfriend, I had finally had a chance to take care of crystal and our children with music, and I did not want to ruin that. That being said, when I got to my mother's apartment, the nice/restrained version of myself threatened to smash her boyfriend's brains out with the hammer if he did not get out of the apartment immediately. And I told him if he ever came back, I would not be bringing a hammer; It would be a gun to finish him off.

Fast forward to about a month or two later—when I found out that my mother's boyfriend went back to my mother's apartment. As promised, I showed up with a gun, he ran out the back door, and somebody else ends up getting shot three times. This is the simple version of the story.

> *"While Worcester police detectives were looking for me for the shooting, they teamed up with Worcester Vice Squad, and the first C-PAC unit to ever exist out in Worcester Massachusetts."*

While Worcester police detectives were looking for me for the shooting, they teamed up with Worcester Vice Squad, and the first C-PAC unit to ever exist out in Worcester Massachusetts. This C-PAC unit just happened to be working with a confidential informant who I was supplying. Previously, he (the confidential informant), who also was a drug dealer and drug user, owed me money and was trying to weasel his way out of paying me back. After threatening to hunt him down and even shoot his daughter, he had absolutely no problem figuring out who he was going to snitch on next. With the help of this confidential informant, I was caught in a drug raid by seven different units. I was charged with attempted murder and drug trafficking. I was raided by seven different units including *FBI, ATF, US Marshals, DEA, State Police, Worcester Detectives,* and *Worcester Vice Squad.* I would later be indicted for a half kilo of cocaine, ecstasy, amitriptyline, a few pounds of marijuana, a gun, and over 300 rounds of ammunition.

> *"Sitting in the police station jail cell, I realized that this was probably the very first time that my entire mind, heart, spirit, and soul had completely come into agreement—at the same exact time—regarding the same exact issue:* **I WAS DONE!***"*

Handcuffs to County Jail

"Therefore, if anyone is in Christ, he is a new creation; old things have passed away; behold, all things have become new" (2 Corinthians 5:17).

Sitting in the police station jail cell, I realized that this was probably the very first time that my entire mind, heart, spirit, and soul had completely come into agreement—at the same exact time—regarding the same exact issue (And yes, I admit that the threats from the *District Attorney's Office* regarding their desire to push for a 20-to-30-year in prison may have had something to do with it.): **I WAS DONE!** You see, I was 22 years old when they took me into custody; it was March 16, 2003. By that time, I had had 15 years in the game, 15 years in the street life, and 15 years of going in and out of the system in some way, shape, or form. Most individuals who end up in jail at the age of 22 (for *"living the street life"*) may have started their negative journey at the age of 17 or 18 years old— which means that they had only been involved with this lifestyle for approximately 4 to 5 years. Even if they started at the tender age of 15 years old—that would still only mean that they had only been involved with the *street life* for approximately 7 years. I had more than double the amount of years with probably four times the amount of crimes committed (if not more), and at this point, I WAS JUST **COMPLETELY DONE!**

PART 2: THE BENEFITS OF A NUTRITIOUS ENVIRONMENT

CHAPTER 5

INTERNAL ENVIRONMENT VS EXTERNAL ENVIRONMENT

*"Walk with the wise and become wise,
for a companion of fools suffers harm."*
(Proverbs 13:20)

Start Where You Are.

In the Bible, Jesus told a story about the *prodigal son*. The story has been read and told over and over again for thousands of years. One of the key moments of the story is when the prodigal son *"came to himself"* *(Luke 15:17)*. In other words, when he came to his senses. It was at that point that the entire direction of his life changed for the better. It is my prayer that you will experience a moment like this before the end of this book—if not, before the end of your life. You see, when a person comes to their senses, they start where they are—*immediately*. They do not wait for their situation or circumstance to change before they *take action*. I was incarcerated in *county jail* and my ability to change my environment was extremely limited. However, I did not allow that to stop me one bit. I changed my external environment by restricting the company that I kept—the people I associated and fellowshipped with— and I changed my internal environment by what I allowed into my mind and spirit—only positive and Godly things (like what I read, watched, and listened to). This type of extreme discipline was *absolutely* necessary during my infant stages of Christianity, healing, growth, and development. You will begin to understand this more thoroughly in the next few chapters of this book.

Completely Done

However, what does *"completely done"* mean and what does it look like; especially, for a 22-year-old young man who is just starting his incarcerated sentence in an environment filled with criminals and sadistic correctional officers? What does *"completely done"* mean and look like for a young man who had not even obtained a high school diploma or licensed trade? More importantly, what does *"completely done"* mean and look like for a young man who has experienced as much abuse, trauma, and neglect as I had— and who was left with such serious scars and triggers? More intensely, what does *"completely done"* mean and look like for a young man who now has to unlearn all of the teachings, philosophies, and perspectives that he was fed over the past 22 years by his father, family, neighborhood, music and movies? The answer to this would require an **ABSOLUTE** renewing of the mind, and completely becoming a *"new person"* (*"new creation"*) so to speak—which I will touch on further in a later chapter. Where does such a young man begin?

> *"With no one to turn to, I turned to the "Master Planner"—GOD."*

With no one to turn to, I turned to the *"Master Planner"—GOD*. Not only did I have to "renew my mind" and become a *"completely different person,"* but I also had to figure out an honest way to take care of my family. Especially, considering the last time that I had turned by back on *my walk* with God—specifically because I had to provide a living for my family (telling God that He would have to understand that my decision to do so was solely to take care them). An individual cannot only address his or her spiritual needs without addressing his or her physical/tangible (worldly) needs as well. In fact, God himself says, *"[a man] who does not provide for [his] relatives, and especially for [his] own household, has denied the faith and is worse than unbeliever"* (1 Timothy 5:8)—and still, *"anyone who has been stealing must steal no longer, but must work doing something useful with their own hands, that they may have something to share with those in need"* (Ephesians 4:28)—and still, *"Suppose a brother or sister is without clothes and daily food. If one of you says to them, 'Go in peace; keep warm and well fed,' but does nothing about their physical needs, what good is it? In the same way, faith by itself, if it is not accompanied by action is dead."* (James 2:15-17) Even Jesus, knowing the spiritual needs of over 5,000 men, women and children (who were following Him), still stopped to make sure that he fed them physical/tangible food before addressing their spiritual needs.

Overall, these two things were the most important for myself:

1.) *An **ABSOLUTE** renewing of the mind, and completely becoming a "new person" so to speak.*

2.) *An honest way to take care of my family.*

Immediately, I already had the answer for number 2 resolved. I was going to do real estate. My uncle had done it, and he had become a millionaire through real estate. (In fact, I was the first person in our family to know that my uncle was a millionaire—when his financial records came out in court during the adoption process for my son because I was in custody and my son's mother was in the streets drinking, drugging, and partying.) I knew I was smart enough to simply follow his instructions, so in my mind, I had already known what I was going to do financially for my family.

The hard part was number 1, and again, where was a young man like myself, with my pedigree, and of my caliber of being, to begin?

> *"Furthermore, these same individuals were living their life in prison the same exact way they were living their life in society..."*

The Chicken Or The Egg?

Typically, when a person thinks about their own environment, they think about the external environment that surrounds them. They think about what is on the outside of a person, external environment, and not about what is on the inside of a person—internal environment. Both the external and internal environment of any human being is extremely important. For example, I would hear individuals in prison talking about the city or town (external environment) in which they had committed their crime in and got arrested in; then, they would say, "when I get out of prison, I'm never coming back to this city or town again"—

as if their incarceration was due to the actions of that city or town (and not due to the fact that they had committed a crime). Furthermore, these same individuals were living their life in prison the same exact way they were living their life in society—still selling drugs, doing drugs, gang banging, etc.. NOTE: If you are reading this book today, in some type of correctional facility, I am here to tell you that you can change your geographical location (external environment)—as many times as you please—but if you do not change your *"self"* (internal environment), you will simply be the same person doing the same things in a different place. Conversely, there were also individuals who knew that changing their internal environment was just as important as changing their external environment—so these individuals worked on *self*:

- Some of them went to church or tried some other type of spiritual enlightenment.
- Some of them worked towards obtaining their GED and/or higher education.
- Some worked on getting trades like a barber's license or CDL license.
- Some worked jobs to develop consistency and job-related skills.
- Some committed to physical workout regimens for their physical and mental health— and self-discipline practices.
- Some attended programs like AA (alcoholics anonymous) and or NA (narcotics anonymous), and other personal development programs as well.

And for the reader who has never been incarcerated, please don't fool yourself into thinking that your internal environment is not as important as your external environment. In fact, you can have more degrees than a thermometer, more wealth than Bill Gates, more fans than Beyoncé, and have traveled to more countries than you can remember—and still be an unhappy, cold hearted, self-absorbed, self-righteous, ignorant bigot. This type of person will never reach their fullest potential as a human, husband or wife, father or mother, son or daughter, sibling, friend, leader, or humanitarian. Therefore, in regards to the internal and external environment of an individual, one might ask the question which is more important and/or which one should be addressed first; thus, the question *"the chicken or the egg?"*

In response to those questions, I would say that both the internal and external environment of an individual are equally important. In other words, if a person were to only change their external environment without at all addressing their internal environment, they should expect the same results—just in a different place (foolishness or some might call it insanity). And if a person were to only work on their internal environment while remaining in an extremely toxic external environ- ment— their progress would be hindered, delayed, and difficult (like swimming upstream). In fact, depending upon how toxic the external environment is, the toxicity of the external environment could prevent all of the growth and development of one's internal environment.

Nonetheless, in regard to which should be addressed first—the internal environment or the external environment— I would say that it would be best to address them both simultaneously for the same exact reasons listed above: focusing on one while neglecting the other, will not produce optimal results.

"The Bible says, "bad company, corrupts good character"
(1 Corinthians 15:33).

The Chicken Or The Egg—Or Both?

In fact, both the internal environment and external environment are one in the same; therefore, working on them both simultaneously is actually the ONLY way to work on them at all. Simply put, what is on the outside, will end up on the inside. In other words, what is on the outside—exterior environment—of a person will end up on the inside—interior environment—of a person. Think of it this way, if you walked into a room and saw 10 complete strangers, you would not be able to measure their character based on their exterior appearance. Thus the saying, "you can't judge a book by its cover." The Bible says, "bad company, corrupts good character" (1 Corinthians 15:33). The "bad company" is on the outside (external environment) of a person and the "good character" that has been affected is on the inside (internal environment) of a person, so what is on the outside ends up on the inside—resulting in them being one in the same. A perfect example of this can be seen in my upbringing; what I was surrounded by in my household (immediate/external environment)—like the anger, violence, etc.—ended up inside of me (and my character so to speak). The same can be said about my neighborhood, the music I listened to, and the movies I watched— what was on the outside ended up on the inside. It is often said that the "eyes and ears are the gateway to the soul," and certain Bible scripture support this saying; I will expand on this a little more in a later chapter. All in all, in response to the famous question, "the chicken or the egg?"— I would argue "both."

Because I was incarcerated, I couldn't just get up and leave the jail in order to change my environment. However, I was able to make decisions to simultaneously address both my internal and external environment. For example, I would only associate with a selected few. More specifically, I stayed away from negativity and individuals who were still doing the same things that had gotten them in prison in the first place. In addition, I did a lot of reading (the Bible and other Christian books), praying, and fasting. Furthermore, I stopped listening to rap music and watching certain programs on television. Overall, I began to allow more of the *positive* into my internal and external environment while doing my very best to keep as much of the *negativity* out of my internal and external environment. And this is when I began to see God work the most.

God's First Lesson

Again, these two things were the most important for myself:

1.) An **ABSOLUTE** renewing of the mind, and completely becoming a "new person" so to speak.

2.) An honest way to take care of my family.

God had made it very clear to me—over the first eight months of my incarceration —that He was definitely going to start with number 1 by teaching me a serious lesson about number 2, and not for the simple, human, limited, sinful reason of "I told you so," but so that He could teach me a lesson that would be in bedded in my soul—so deep and so strong—for the purpose of never being able to be tricked by the devil again regarding the *provision* of my family. In other words, God does command a man to provide for his family, but He does not want us breaking the law, committing crimes, cutting corners, compromising, and sinning against Himself and/or others in order to do so. And that, however, is exactly what I had done when I had chosen to turn my back on my *walk with God,* so I could simply provide for my family.

"Therefore I tell you, do not worry about your life, what you will eat or drink; or about your body, what you will wear. Is not life more than food, and the body more than clothes? Look at the birds of the air; they do not sow or reap or store away in barns, and yet your heavenly Father feeds them. Are you not much more valuable than they? Can any one of you by worrying add a single hour to your life? "And why do you worry about clothes? See how the flowers of the field grow. They do not labor or spin. Yet I tell you that not even Solomon in all his splendor was dressed like one of these. If that is how God clothes the grass of the field, which is here today and tomorrow is thrown into the fire, will he not much more clothe you—you of little faith? So do not worry, saying, 'What shall we eat?' or 'What shall we drink?' or 'What shall we wear?' For the pagans run after all these things, and your heavenly Father knows that you need

them. But seek first his kingdom and his righteousness, and all these things will be given to you as well. Therefore do not worry about tomorrow, for tomorrow will worry about itself. Each day has enough trouble of its own" (Matthew 6:25-34 NIV)

There is no question about it; I immediately started to "seek first" the kingdom of God and "His righteousness." I started right there in the police station jail cell—on my knees— praying to God. There is no question at all regarding the why—I was being threatened with 20 to 30 years in prison. So, I started seeking Him "hard-core"—so to speak. What started as intense prayer in the police station jail cell only continued with momentum once I reached county jail. It was there that I was able to get my hands on a Bible and start to combine my prayer life with reading His Word, fasting, and doing my best to live what I was learning.

One can only imagine what my biggest concern was—the very thing that the devil had used in previous times to get me to turn my back on *my walk* with God. Yes, you guessed right, the provision of crystal and our children. However, now I was equipped with God's promises in the Bible, and I had read, *"I was young and now I am old, yet I have never seen the righteous forsaken or their children begging bread"* (Psalms 37:25 NIV). This actually became one of my favorite Bible scriptures. I read it and repeated it often—and continued to *"seek first"* the kingdom of God and *"his righteousness."*

Crystal did not have a job or any type of income, and she spent most of her time at home—taking care of our three children who were 1, 3 and 5 years old at the time. I remember experiencing lots of anxiety because I was incarcerated and could not provide a single penny for my family. To make matters worse, the landlord of the apartment building that we lived in had heard about my crimes and began to threaten to evict my wife and kids from the apartment. The feds had taken all the drugs and money—and all of my so-called friends had disappeared.

Furthermore, my father was also incarcerated, along with all three of my brothers, and my mother and extended family was broke— struggling enough to take care of their own families and make ends meet (and my younger sister was only 14 years old at the time). As you can imagine, all of the above-mentioned details only increased my anxiety.

> *"Realizing that God did not want his children to live in anxiety, I begin to pray that God would provide for my family in my absence."*

Then I came across a scripture that read, *"Do not be anxious about anything, but in every situation, by prayer and petition, with thanksgiving, present your requests to God. And the peace of God, which transcends all understanding, will guard your hearts and your minds in Christ Jesus. Finally, brothers and sisters, whatever is true, whatever is noble, whatever is right, whatever is pure, whatever is lovely, whatever is admirable—if anything is excellent or praiseworthy—think about such things"* (Philippians 4:6-8 NIV). Realizing that God did not want his children to live in anxiety, I began to pray that God would provide for my family in my absence. Crystal was informed that she could get some type of government assistance, but she would first have to go into a homeless shelter, receive welfare and section 8, and wait on the system to provide some type of housing. She was scared to death, afraid of going into a homeless shelter, and could not even imagine having to experience it with her children. Because of this, I prayed specific prayers, "God please allow the rent to be paid." I knew she could get food-stamps to feed herself and the kids and even get food from local "food banks," so my prayers were specifically for rent money. In doing so, I was presenting my *"prayer and petition"* to God, and I would thank him (*"with thanksgiving"*) as if it was already done. I would notice that the anxiety would disappear, and *"the peace of God, which transcends all understanding, [began to] guard [my] heart and [my] mind in Christ Jesus"* (Philippians 4:6, 7 NIV). In addition, I begin to think good thoughts—*"Finally, brothers and sisters, whatever is true, whatever is noble, whatever is right, whatever is pure, whatever is lovely, whatever is admirable—if anything is excellent or praiseworthy—think about such things*" (Philippians 4:8 NIV). This type of thinking only enhanced the peace that I was experiencing. Long story short, the first of the month arrived, and the rent was paid in full. A few dollars from here, a few dollars from there, a few dollars from this person, a few dollars from that person. God had answered my prayer.

Immediately, the devil swooped in with all types of lies and doubts saying, "this was not God; it was just a coincidence; just wait and see what happens next month." However, I simply continued to "*seek first*" the kingdom of God and "*His righteousness,*" presenting my "*prayers and petitions*" to God—thanking him in advance for hearing and answering my prayers— allowing His peace that "*transcends all understanding*" to guard my heart and mind, and I continued to focus on positive thoughts.

> "*Immediately, the devil swooped in with all types of lies and doubts saying, 'this was not God; it was just a coincidence; just wait and see what happens next month.'*"

In short, month two of my incarceration, and the rent was paid in full again. Once again, the devil would try to bombard my thoughts with doubts and fear— using the same lies and making the same statements—"this was not God; it was just a coincidence; just wait and see what happens next month." Month three of my incarceration, and the rent was paid in full again. Then, God gave me a *Revelation* and a *Rhema Word*—He had spoken to me clearly and directly, He said, "son, right now you are in a cell, and you cannot provide a single penny for your family, and *I AM* providing everything." He said, "son, you could have kept your job at UPS—providing *something* (versus nothing) for your wife and children—and I, simply, would have provided the rest. You did not have to turn your back on your *walk with Me* in order to provide for your family." This *Revelation* and *Rhema Word* from God hit me like a ton of bricks—realizing that all I had to do was trust God and do the very thing that I was doing in jail, which was—continue to *"seek first"* the kingdom of God and *"His righteousness,"* present my *"prayers and petitions"* to God, thank Him in advance for hearing and answering my prayers, allow His peace that *"transcends all understanding"* to guard my heart and mind, and continue to focus on positive thoughts. As you can imagine, the devil was not finished with me, but the good news was that God was not finished with me either.

> *"As you can imagine, the devil was not finished with me, but the good news was that God was not finished with me either."*

As expected, the devil began singing the same old song again, "this was not God; it was just a coincidence; just wait and see what happens next month." Month four of my incarceration, and the rent was paid in full again. This happened month after month; money would just randomly appear from different sources. So much so, that I had finally just spoken back to the devil and said, "you might as well give up Homie because there is no way that you can convince me that this is a coincidence." I had read far too many scriptures and promises from God that talked about God's unfailing provision for his children's needs. So, I just continued to *"seek first"* the kingdom of God and *"His righteousness,"* present my *"prayers and petitions"* to God, thank Him in advance for hearing and answering my prayers, allow His peace that *"transcends all understanding"* to guard my heart and mind, and continued to focus on positive thoughts. As a result, the rent got paid every month in full for a total of eight months straight. Then, after 8 months, the money just completely stopped. Crystal's mother had stopped traveling the world with her husband and the Navy—and had finally settled down and purchased a home in California. Crystal and the kids moved in with her mother and was finally in a safe and stable environment. It was during these first 8 months of my incarceration, where God had begun an ABSOLUTE renewing of my mind—starting the process of me completely becoming a "new creation."

One might be asking his or herself, "what was Nick doing exactly—in regards to seeking "first" the kingdom of God and "His righteousness?" Well, I literally put Him first—as soon as I would open my eyes every morning— I would begin to talk to God and spend time with Him in prayer (relationship). I would thank Him for being alive, thank Him for protecting and providing for my family, and I would spend time reading His Word, the Bible. While reading His Word, I would learn about how He wanted me to live my life, so I would do my best to follow the things that I was reading (obedience). For example, I learned that I should forgive, pray for my enemies, and be kind to others. So, I would do my best to be obedient in these areas, and if I ever struggled in any specific area, I would simply ask God for help, and He would provide it. I once heard a very wise man say that "Jesus was a simple man with a simple plan." God keeps things very simple for us—not providing a large spotlight to see clearly into the future, but always providing a flashlight to see our next step on the pathway.

As I adjusted my external environment to keep the negativity out—and as I adjusted my internal environment which allowed positivity in (through the Bible and other Christian books)—a process of growth, learning, faith, trust, education, and miracles began to take place right before my very eyes.

Being Used By God

During my time in county jail from 2003 to 2006 (approximately 3 years) God had begun to use me. Although I chose to stay to myself, and only associate with a handful of people, both inmates and correctional officers were watching me.

(Note: Always be aware of those who are watching you. Whether you realize it or not, there is always someone watching you. They would see me leave the block/unit and go to every church service, and every Bible study that was announced and available. Other men who were also incarcerated would attend such church services and Bible studies as well. Some of them were serious about their belief and others, simply, wanted to leave the block/unit that they were in to either experience some mobility, or to see a friend or family member who was in another block/unit. However, both the correctional officers and inmates knew who was serious about their belief in God—and who was not. And this was solely because they watched carefully and paid close attention to others on a regular basis. Someone is always watching.)

Because I was doing my best to live a life that was obedient to God's Word, this was seen and noticed in my every day *walk* in life. So when I approached the leader of a gang called the *Latin Kings* after a vicious, bloody, jail fight— God's Holy Spirit, gave me the words to say to lead that man to *Salvation*. This individual denounced his gang, turned to Christ, began going to church, and surrendered his life to God.

"As the conversation continued, I could see his certainty start to diminish, and his curiosity arise."

There was another young man who was in jail for murder, and he called himself an atheist. As God used me to witness and minister to this individual—who had a bunch of beliefs and reasons to believe that God just was not real at all— God showed me in my spirit that this young man simply had questions he never felt safe enough to ask. I later learned that the only reason why this young man felt safe enough to ask me certain questions is because he too had been watching me live my life in jail for approximately two years. The conversation started with his certainty that God was not real and with questions he just knew I would not be able to answer, but as God spoke to my spirit and spoke through my words, I was able to give a gentle answer to every question he presented. As the conversation continued, I could see his certainty start to diminish, and his curiosity arise. Then God began to do something super naturally. As God spoke to this young man—through me—He (God) would reveal to me additional questions that this man had but did not verbalize. So, as I continued to speak, I began to answer questions that were in this young man's mind—before he asked them. This continued—"*in real time*"—throughout the remainder of the conversation. As a result, this young man gave his life to Christ, denounced his atheism, and begin attending church services in county jail. *To GOD Be ALL The Glory!*

There were many situations, throughout my 3 years in county jail, in which God would use me in a one-on-one conversation to witness and minister to an individual. He (God) would give me the words to say—with a supernatural insight—combined with my willingness to be submissive to God's *Holy Spirit*, and the experiences were always amazing. There were times when I would be in a *bullpen (holding tank/cell)* with about 20 to 30 other men, and I would begin witnessing to one individual. The place would be so loud—correctional officers yelling at inmates, inmates yelling at correctional officers, men yelling at their attorneys, and men laughing and telling stories— while others were selling drugs and using drugs. I would notice—while witnessing and ministering to one individual— that the man to his right would start listening in, which meant that there was one less person making noise. Shortly after, the man to his left, would start listening in—resulting in one less person making noise. This would go on until the entire *bullpen* was quiet and I was the only person speaking—about God. God did this on a few different occasions, and I would be blown away—knowing that these men were not listening to me, but listening to the Spirit of God within me. And I would just love the fact that God would use *me* to speak to these men.

> *"There was one time in particular when God's Spirit had come upon me, with a Holy Boldness."*

There was one time in particular when God's *Spirit* had come upon me, with a *Holy Boldness.* Two men, a white man and a black man, with *shanks* (knives/blades) in their hands were about to stab each other in a fight. The Spirit of God came upon me, and I stepped in the middle of these two men. As they continued towards each other, I placed one hand on the white man's chest and placed my other hand on the black man's chest. As they continued towards each other, I held them both apart with my arms. Believing that the distance was not far enough, I extended my leg and put my foot on one man's chest, while my hand was on the other man's chest. Probably looking like an ancient martial arts monk, I stood there, standing on 1 foot, until both men put their *shanks* away and walked away. After later speaking to both men, individually, they both had expressed that the only reason why they did not start slashing away was because it was *me.* They both had expressed in some form or fashion that they had recognized me as a *real man of God*—because they too had been watching how I was living my life in county jail. This was extremely humbling to myself because I was only around 24 years old at the time. They even placed an emphasis on the fact that if I had not stepped in the middle of them, they would have stabbed the other man. They also made it clear to me that if it were anyone else who had stepped in the middle of them, that person would have gotten stabbed as well. Again, I say, to God be ALL the Glory.

These examples display the fruit an individual can experience when he or she maximizes the control of his or her own interior and exterior environment—displaying how the changes first take place within the individual, and then overflow to the point of changing the environment outside/around the individual. Also, displaying how we are all interconnected, and how the internal and external environment of a person are also intertwined and interconnected.

CHAPTER 6

A CONTROLLED ENVIRONMENT

"The righteous choose their friends carefully,
but the way of the wicked leads them astray."
(Proverbs 12:26)

Re-potted From Facility to Facility to Facility

Imagine with me, if you will, a small plant placed in a kitchen windowsill. As the plant is watered and receives the sunlight, it grows too big for the pot that it is in. So the owner finds a larger pot, fills it with good soil, but the pot is too big for the windowsill. So it now gets placed on the kitchen counter. As the plant continues to grow, it outgrows its pot again, so the owner finds a larger pot and now places it in the living room. With plenty of water and lots of sunlight, the plant gets too big for the living room. The owner finds a larger pot, fills it with good soil, and places the plant outside on the front porch. The plant continues to grow—so big and so beautiful—that the owner decides to re-plant it out in the forest, where it eventually grows to its fullest potential.

At first glance, this appears to be an amazing story about a plant being able to reach its fullest potential. However, at every stage of growth, this plant experienced different dangers, and as the plant grew from one stage to another, the dangers the plant experienced also grew in severity. For example, when the plant was in a small pot, sitting in the windowsill, it seemed to be completely free of most dangers—out of the reach of children, constantly in the owner's view (which reminded the owner to keep it watered), and receiving the full sun light of day. In fact, the only true danger that the plant was experiencing was the hindrance of growth due to the small pot it was kept in. Once re-potted in a larger pot and placed on the kitchen counter, the plant would experience an occasional splash of hot soapy water from the kitchen sink and would occasionally experience being bumped or brushed up against by some-one reaching into the kitchen cupboards that were directly over the kitchen counter. Being re-potted in a larger pot and placed in the living room, only seemed like a great promotion. However, the living room often had the most traffic. It's where the kids would play with their toys, and the family would gather for game nights and movie nights. The living room was also the place where all their friends and extended family would gather. As a result of the heavy traffic and activity, the plant got knocked over a few times. It lost a few leaves, it lost some soil, and it's roots were momentarily disturbed. However, against all odds, and with some *TLC* (Tender Loving Care) from its owner, the plant just continued to grow. So much so that the owner re-potted the plant, in a much larger pot, and decided to place the plant out on the front porch.   At this point, the plant is subject to insects, changing temperatures, winds and weather, but somehow it just continued to grow. Lastly, the plant is placed in the forest—where it received all the best natural ingredients to grow and flourish—with lots of space for its roots to dig deep, spread, and expand. Nevertheless, the forest is also where it experienced the greatest dangers—but somehow, the dangers that could not destroy the plant, only made it stronger and taller—becoming more useful and purposeful than it had ever been before. You see, not only did this plant turn into a fruitful tree, but it had also become a shelter and resting place for other living organisms like birds, insects, and other creatures of nature as well.

"This re-potting experience continues to repeat itself throughout the entirety of a person's life..."

So, as God re-potted me from county jail to a state prison classification facility —*MCI CONCORD*—then, to *MCI NORFOLK* prison (where individuals stay to complete their prison sentences and/or spend the rest of their natural lives), each re-potting process allowed me to experience dangers that could have killed me (but instead only made me stronger) and nutrients for growth and development. The re-potting process is never a comfortable one, but it is *essential* for growth and development. Just think when you were a freshman in high school; it was new, uncomfortable, scary, intimidating. By the next year, as a sophomore, you felt a little more comfortable in your own skin and in your educational development. By the time you were a junior in high school, you started to feel like you had finally figured things out. And by your senior year, you were "the man" or "the woman" feeling like you had mastered high school only to be re-potted again into college as a freshman. Again, things feeling new, uncomfortable, scary, and intimidating as a freshman in college—and having to repeat this re-potting process from freshman to sophomore, sophomore to junior, and junior to senior in college. This re-potting experience continues to repeat itself throughout the entirety of a person's life—the first few years in a career, the first few years of marriage, the first few years as a parent, the first few years parenting a teenager, the first few years parenting a young adult, the first few years of your 30s, the first few years of your 40s, the first few years of your 50s, the first few years of your 60s, etc.

> *"So, as God re-potted me from facility to facility to facility, each repotting experience had its dangers that were new, uncomfortable, scary, and intimidating..."*

So, as God re-potted me from *facility to facility to facility*, each repotting experience had its dangers that were new, uncomfortable, scary, and intimidating—along with its nourishments that were healing, exciting, inspiring and uplifting. For example, county jail was filled with a bunch of *knuckleheads*, who would continually come in and out of jail due to petty crimes and small sentences— so it was so much easier to get in trouble if you associated with the wrong individuals. County jail *"dangers"* also included the limitation of resources—like books and educational opportunities—which resulted in less people doing good. Once re-potted to *MCI Concord*, the classification facility, the dangers increased—much more violence (fights and stabbings and deaths) and gang activity. Individuals were angry because they were recently convicted and sentenced to time in prison. They were also scared with *"something to prove"*— a more dog eat dog environment. However, *MCI Concord* had a GED program, more access to books and a library, personal development programs, and religious programs— which resulted in a few more people attempting to do right in a much more dangerous environment. Then, there was *MCI Norfolk*—the greatest danger there was a *spirit of hopelessness* that was strong enough to consume any individual who did not have God on his side. You see, *MCI Norfolk* was the prison that had the most *"lifers"* in a single facility in the entire state. *"Lifers"* were individuals who were sentenced to life in prison. Some *lifers* were sentenced for the crime of second-degree murder, which meant their sentences were *15 years to life*. Other *lifers* were sentenced for the crime of first-degree murder, which meant their sentences were *life in prison without the possibility of parole*. I was sent to this prison because I had a *15 year minimum mandatory sentence* for drug trafficking. *MCI Norfolk*, on the flipside, had much more *freedom* (less cell time), and lots of programs, activities, educational opportunities, trade licensing, and religious programs. It was here, at *MCI Norfolk*, where I experienced the majority of my development during the time that I was incarcerated. I met Christian men with integrity and character— men who wanted to see other men succeed—men who were not afraid to smile because they were not just confident in themselves, but confident in their God. Men who completely put aside the *tough guy* façade and were willing to laugh with you and cry with you. It was with these men that I learned how to socialize. Before meeting these men, I very seldomly smiled in public, or in any correctional facility that I was held in. I kept a straight face, always vigilant, always being aware of my surroundings, and not trusting anyone who was around me. It was around these men that I felt safe to be myself safe to socialize. So, I surrounded myself with men like this throughout the remainder of my incarceration. Most importantly, God promises to put people in our lives to bless us—these promises can be found all throughout the Bible, including *Isaiah 43:4*.

> *"Simply put, I got myself in the room with the best of the best regarding everything that I pursued while incarcerated."*

The Best of The Best

Simply put, I got myself in the room with the *best of the best* regarding everything that I pursued while incarcerated. In fact, I did not only get in the room with the *best*, I sat at their table by specific invite and created long lasting relationships with them. And this not by sneaky and deceptive ways, but by a sincere desire to learn and ask questions. They might say, "it was Nick's confidence," "the questions he asked," or "there's just something about him." I would say it was the favor of God granting me favor with them. Finding men like this, who could contribute to my healing and development, was exciting, inspiring and uplifting. For whatever reason, God has blessed me with a spirit of discernment; I have always been able to identify the *best of the best*. Even, in regard to the negative life of crime, I could always identify who was the best at what they were doing —and they would be the people who I chose to learn from. This is also the reason why all of my closest friends today are individuals who are much older than myself—*ENVIRONMENT*.

1). The Best of The Best: In The Church

So, upon my arrival at *MCI Norfolk*, the first place I wanted to be was in church and around like-minded individuals. Within the first few months of my arrival, I had identified who was who and what was what in this small church environment. You see, there are those who try to look super spiritual, and there are those who are the real deal. There are those who try to look wise, and there are those who are actually wise. There are those who try to look like leaders, and there are those who are legitimate leaders. Surrounding myself with other spiritual giants only expedited my spiritual growth and development. Just as the Bible says, "iron sharpens iron," these men played a major role in the growth and development of my faith and walk with Christ. These men saw my potential, embraced me, and made me one of their own. They helped point out both my strengths and weaknesses— always supporting, always encouraging, and even rebuking if and when necessary. They made me a part of their team for the purpose of doing good. They taught me how to be an agent for change. They taught me how to use my pain and story/testimony to help others—not just in the church and secular programs, but in everyday life. They helped me see (with my own eyes) what God had been telling me for years—that "my pain had a purpose."

2.) *The Best of The Best: In 2ⁿᵈ Thoughts Inc.*

I would later spend *a year and some change* healing and developing while being counseled and trained to enter into a program called *2nd Thoughts Inc.* where we would mentor *at risk* youth who were getting in trouble with the law. Although this was a secular program, it was run and facilitated by a group of Christian men. So, although we could not *preach* to the youth about God, we could always give them Godly counsel. The board members of this program not only counselled youth, but they had been counseling men for years and were seasoned in their ability to get results. Being limited to a certain number of sessions/weeks to work with men both young and old, they were strategic, skilled, experienced, and effective. They were strategic in asking questions with an ability to pull information out of a man that he did not even know was down inside of himself. My quick summary of their abilities and expertise is an understatement. These men were good at what they did—and, as a young man, I got to sit at their table and eat off of their many years of experience.

> *"By the grace of God, and with lots of studying, I scored high enough to earn a four-year scholarship from Boston University..."*

3.) *The Best of The Best: In Boston University*

By the grace of God, and with lots of studying, I scored high enough to earn a four-year scholarship from *Boston University*—while incarcerated. I was being taught by college professors from *Boston University, Harvard,* and *Lasell College.* My study partner was a white privileged kid who went to private schools growing up. He was also incarcerated for drug trafficking because he was a rebellious young man who *wanted his own stuff that he bought with his own money*. His name was Luis, and he was clearly the smartest kid in the class. I would spend two whole weeks working on a final paper, and I would watch this kid bang out his paper—handwritten—within an hour of having to turn it in, and he would always get an "A." There were two other white kids who were at the top of our class (they were friends who sat side-by-side). Both also from privileged backgrounds—one was in prison because he had gotten drunk after a party and got into a car accident that had killed someone—not sure what his friend was in for. Both these guys would always try to compete with Luis (my study partner) in every class—regarding who got the highest grade. But they were no match for Luis. Luis' grade would always be a few points higher than theirs. I was just thankful to be in college. I would pray before class, pray in class, and pray after class. I would pray while I was studying, I would pray while writing a paper, I would pray before an exam—during the exam—and after the exam. When the professors were giving us back our graded quizzes, exams, or papers, I would always flip it upside down and wait until I got back to my cell before looking at the grade (also, praying before I looked at it). Thinking back, it makes me laugh. Eventually, Luis would come around and ask me about my grade, and I would say, "I did OK." He would say, "can I see"? Then, I would show him the grade—which was almost always identical to his. He would smile, punch me in the shoulder and say, yeah right—you did ok." I would try to hold back my smile, but inside, I was doing cartwheels and backflips. It makes sense that our grades were identical almost *all of the time*, right? I mean, he was my study partner. The only difference was that he would study for about a half hour and I would study for a whole week. I have a lot of thanks and gratitude towards Luis that I do not think I ever properly expressed to him. He would always stop whatever he was doing to answer any questions I had regarding any assignment I was working on. There were a few times—during our study sessions— that I would point out something he missed. He would say, "wow, thanks Nick." Then, after the exam, we would get our grades, and they would be identical again. One time, Luis got mad at his two white friends (the two who were always trying to compete with him) for making a comment about why I always flip my papers over— assuming that I did so because I was ashamed of my grades.

> *"I also knew that there were other minorities in the room who did not have a privileged white friend to study with."*

Luis got so mad that he snatched my paper and put it in their faces saying, "look he got the highest grade in the class." They both were shocked and felt pretty foolish. Luis later apologized to me for doing that, but I told him, "Don't worry about it, it kind of felt good." In reality, flipping my paper over was a way for me to try to remain humble. I have always been competitive, but I was trying to not be cocky and conceited like Luis and his two friends. I also knew that there were other minorities in the room who did not have a privileged white friend to study with. I would try to help others when I could, but understanding the material was hard enough on myself—feeling like school was draining every ounce of my being. Moral of the story is, a student is only as good as his teacher. If you learn from fools, you will become a fool. Even the Bible says, that the "blind cannot lead the blind," (Luke 6:39). And I will add, if you want to be average, learn from and surround yourself with average people. But if you want to be considered amongst the best, learn from and surround yourself with the best—wherever you currently may be (even in prison), so when your time comes to be repotted in a bigger and better—more nutritious—environment, you will be ready for that environment with the plans to repeat the same process of seeking out the best of the best. Get yourself around some better people.

> *"MCI Norfolk was the most privileged medium security prison facility in all of Massachusetts."*

4.) The Best of The Best: In The Gym

MCI Norfolk was the most privileged *medium security* prison facility in all of Massachusetts. More specifically, their weight-room/workout gymnasium was fitting for any professional bodybuilder and/or strength trainer/power lifter. Whether you have experienced prison yourself—or have only seen it in movies and/or television shows—what you have seen and experienced is nothing compared to the obsession with fitness, bodybuilding, and powerlifting that the inmates at *MCI Norfolk* had embodied in the environment of their weight-room. Because of the facility's privileges, inmates were able to order as many books and magazines regarding health, fitness, bodybuilding, and strength training (power lifting) as they desired. Viewing our *canteen list* was like viewing an itemize list from a grocery store. Individuals were able to purchase and cook meats like chicken and ground beef—and have access to so many other food and beverage items. They were able to grow their own vegetables and could purchase protein shakes by the caseload. Not to mention every year was a professional powerlifting competition in which the judges came in from the *"outside world"* and set up the lights and competition stage for the main three lifts: *bench-press, squat,* and *dead lift.* The champions—if their numbers were high enough for their weight class—would end up in the same magazines that so many subscribers were reading each month. Some of the competitors were *lifers* and others were not. Surrounded by a wealth of knowledge in every weight class—along with every muscle magazine and book about powerlifting, bodybuilding, diet and exercise—you can already imagine who I went to for advice to discuss strategy and technique. Yes, you guessed it—*"the best of the best."* Surrounding myself with individuals who were obsessed with the mysteries and science of health, fitness, strength, and muscle development, only maximized my experience in the gym. I had come to learn and understand *my body* so intricately that I could do whatever I wanted with my body. I had once read that *Will Smith*— after gaining approximately 100 pounds of muscle to play the character *Muhammad Ali* in the movie *Ali*, had to later shed that weight to play in other movies including *I am legend*— said that he can do whatever he wanted with his body. I momentarily fell in love with that concept, and—just like Will—I too could do whatever I wanted with my body.

> *"I momentarily fell in love with that concept, and—just like Will—I too could do whatever I wanted with my body."*

I won my first competition by default because the two other men in my weight class were so competitive that they kept increasing their numbers—on paper—for their first lift, simply, to compete with one another. Both individuals failed on their first attempts, and I had known enough to know that after tapping into their *central nervous system* on their first attempts, success with their second and third lifts would be close to impossible—and I was right. As a result, neither individual in my weight class was able to put a number on the board, so I won by default. It was my first competition, and I had no plans on actually competing (applying effort). I had only entered the competition because a mentor of mine suggested that I should do so for experience, and to see what the whole competition environment was like. My plans were to compete in the following competition and win. At the time, I had had a 365 pound bench—with a controlled pause— not bouncing it off my chest. My first lift was for 225 pounds. It felt like a feather back then. I could bench 225 pounds between 20 to 30 reps at a time. Since the other two gentlemen had failed on their first attempts, I simply repeated those numbers—225 pounds for my second lift and 225 pounds for my third lift. That's all that was needed to win the competition. But again, I was not there to win my first time around. Shortly after the competition, I had bet a couple of friends that I could *shred up* and lose a tremendous amount of weight in a 90 day period. The bet was on, and the results immediately followed—goal accomplished. Being shredded and nicely chiseled at 188 pounds felt good and looked amazing, but there is just something about having size and power in prison. So, it wasn't long before I started hitting the steel again, extremely hard, and using both my bodybuilding and strengthening training techniques to gain excessive muscle mass. I had mastered the understanding of my body so well that rumors started to spread throughout the prison that I had access to steroids. Overall, placing myself in an environment with *the best of the best* gave me access to a wealth of knowledge and experience—as well as access to some of the best reading material regarding diet, exercise, bodybuilding, and strength training. ENVIRONMENT IS CRUCIAL!

The Chinese Baby Concept

I came up with this concept that I call the *Chinese Baby Concept*—if you took a Chinese baby and placed it into an African-American home as an infant, and then raised that child in the African-American home for the first 21 years of its life, that child would *walk black, talk black, eat black*, etc. The child's *style, swag,* and mannerisms would all resemble the African-American culture. In fact, some have seen this on many occasions when a Caucasian family has adopted an Asian child, and the child grows up speaking English without any Asian accent at all. I share that to share this—in the same way, if you took a fool and only surrounded that fool with wise individuals, the fool would become wise accidentally. Just imagine if he applied himself, just imagine if he wanted to learn, just imagine if he wanted to do better and be better—just imagine.

"In other words, in a controlled environment, I still had to control my environment—both internally and externally."

The Prison Promise

While I was being re-potted from facility to facility to facility—during those eight years of my incarceration—I was growing roots that started growing longer, deeper, and stronger, and in each place, I had to do my best to control my environment. In other words, in a *controlled environment*, I still had to control my environment—both internally and externally. And one of the things that had become extremely apparent to myself was the fact that my growth was coming from and was intertwined with the people and information (*ENVIRONMENT*) that I was exposed to— *intentionally.* Thus, the prison promise—I had promised myself that when I get out of prison, I am only going to surround myself with people who are *better than me.* More specifically, in regards to everything that I wanted to achieve and/or become, I would specifically find individuals in that field who were the *best of the best,* so I could improve in that specific area of my life. Just as in my *incarcerated life,* whether in church, *2nd Thoughts Inc., Boston University,* or the gym, I surrounded myself with people who were better than me (*the best of the best*)—people who were more experienced and had more knowledge regarding the subject at hand—maximizing my potential for optimal growth.

> *"I had called my grandmother and told her that I had been sentenced to 15 to 17 years in prison, and my grandmother's first response with absolute confidence and no hesitation was, 'THE DEVIL IS A LIE!'"*

God's Promise & Preparation: Expansion Before Promotion

Before being sentenced to a 15-to-17-year prison sentence with the first 15 years being a *minimum mandatory* sentence, God had spoken to my spirit and told me that he was never going to allow me to do 15 years in prison. He also gave me specific and timely confirmation twice: once, before being sentenced to a 15 to 17 year prison sentence, and once after being sentenced to a 15 to 17 year prison sentence. Both confirmations came with complete agreement in my spirit—complete rest, peace, and comfort— without any trace of fear, doubt, or unbelief. The first confirmation came through my father. I told him that the district attorney's office was threatening me with 20 to 30 years in prison, and I asked him if I should take a deal. His response was, "absolutely not." I then explained to him that if I did not take a deal, and was found guilty in trial, I would have to serve a minimum of 15 years in prison. He then said—with absolute confidence and no hesitation— "son, God is not going to allow you to do 15 years in prison. He is just using this time to draw you closer to Him; just seek His face, and He will do the rest." I received that word and confirmation from God with complete agreement in my spirit—complete rest, peace, and comfort— without any trace of fear, doubt, or unbelief. I believed God's promise all the way through trial, and throughout the entirety of my prison sentence. More specifically, when I was found guilty in trial—and sentenced to 15 to 17 years in prison with the first 15 years being a *minimum mandatory* prison sentence—while watching my mother cry, I had so much peace and confidence (with a smile on my face) when I turned to my mother and said, "Ma, don't worry; I am not doing 15 years in prison" as the correctional officers/bailiffs walked me off (in handcuffs) to the holding cell.

> *"There was a season while incarcerated at MCI Norfolk, that the idea of my freedom had a lingering sense of urgency."*

The second confirmation, also timely, came from my grandmother (my father's mother) after being sentenced to 15 to 17 years in prison. I had just been shipped—*re-potted*—from county jail to upstate prison at *MCI Concord* in Massachusetts. I had called my grandmother and told her that I had been sentenced to 15 to 17 years in prison, and my grandmother's first response with absolute confidence and no hesitation was, *"THE DEVIL IS A LIE!"* I do not remember anything else that was said during that phone call, but I do know that I received that word and confirmation from God with complete agreement in my spirit—complete rest, peace, and comfort— without any trace of fear, doubt, or unbelief.

In a later conversation with my grandfather (my mother's father) over the phone, he began to share with me that he was old and did not believe that he would still be alive at the end of my 15-year prison sentence. I, in turn, with absolute confidence and no hesitation, shared with him that I would not be doing 15 years in prison. My grandfather was not too big on faith, so I am not sure if he believed me or not. The truth of the matter is, when God has given you a promise, even amongst great people of faith— some will believe with you and others will doubt. My father would make bold statements of *faith*, first, and then ask you if you wanted to be a part of a miracle—by believing with him. He would say, if you believe with him, you will take part in a miracle, but if you doubt and do not believe, he will still receive the miracle, but you lost the opportunity to be a part of that miracle. And he *believed* what he said—no pun intended. That, my friends, is *relentless* faith.

There was a season while incarcerated at *MCI Norfolk*, that the idea of my freedom had a lingering sense of urgency. This sense of urgency was so strong that I couldn't keep it to myself. In the hopes of receiving some support, agreement, encouragement, and advise, I shared it with a few Christian brothers and a small handful of associates who were in my immediate circle. To my surprise, not a single person believed me. In fact, I had told a beloved friend/*brother in Christ, Thomas Koonce,* that I would be leaving soon (getting out of prison).

> *"It is important for even believers to surround themselves with other faith filled believers, who have similar or higher faith levels..."*

He knew that I was sentenced to a 15-to-17-year prison sentence (with the first 15 years being a *minimum mandatory* sentence), so he would ask questions like, "did you receive good news from your attorney." When I would say, "no," he would say, "so how do you know that you are getting out soon." I would try to explain to him that it was a "God thing," but he never seemed convinced—which prevented him from genuinely being happy with me and for me. God had shown me in the spiritual realm that Tommy was looking for something tangible —in the natural world— which is actually the opposite of faith. The Bible says, "*Now faith is the substance of things hoped for, the evidence of things not seen*" (Hebrews 11:1 NKJV). I would jokingly call Tommy "*doubting Thomas*"— like the Thomas in the Bible who seen Jesus's dead body on the cross, and seen Him buried in the tomb, and refused to believe that He (Jesus) had risen from the dead—until he (Thomas) could personally put his fingers in the holes of Jesus's hands and in the hole of Jesus's side. And Jesus's response to Thomas was, "*Thomas, because you have seen Me, you have believed. Blessed are those who have not seen and yet have believed*" (John 20:29 NKJV). As the reader, you are probably wondering what any of this has to do with environment. Well, it has everything to do with environment. It is important for even believers to surround themselves with other faith filled believers, who have similar or higher faith levels—individuals who do not necessarily need to see something in the natural in order to believe it in faith. Being around doubting individuals can slowly eat away at your faith and cause you to doubt. Going forward, I had to be strategic about what I shared with Tommy. If people cannot get on your faith level, you will have to leave them behind. Is it better to please God or man? If God is expanding your faith to believe for more—so you can move into your *Promised Land*—it would be foolish of you to shrink down to a lower level of faith to appease others (and to have the company of those whose faith cannot rise to the occasion) and forfeit the very blessing that awaits you. I chose to believe God and walk in faith—and, in doing so, I had to leave Tommy and the other Christian brothers at *MCI Norfolk* behind—both spiritually (faith-wise) and literally, as I would soon after be released back into society.

Don't get me wrong, I love my brother Tommy dearly, and to-day (approximately 15 years later) we can both attest to the fact that Tommy's faith has grown tremendously. In fact, God would later use me to speak a prophetic *Word* to Tommy at a time of desperate need. A specific *rhema Word* with five very specific details which all came to pass very quickly and before our very eyes. You see, Tommy was sentenced to a *natural life sentence*—life in prison without the possibility of parole. After serval failed motions and appeals to the *Superior Courts*—and even an appeal to the Governor's Office for a pardon and/or commutation—Tommy had served 30 years in prison. In 2022, after Massachusetts Governor *Baker* announced his resignation, he granted Tommy a commutation which had to be approved by 8 members of the Governor's Council. I, along with many others, was blessed with the opportunity to speak highly of Tommy during that all day event. Thomas Koonce is an amazing human being, son, brother, father, uncle, cousin, leader, and—most importantly—Christian. In short, he spent 30 years in prison helping people (spiritually, mentally, emotionally, educationally, etc.) and created and operated programs that have left everlasting impressions on the lives of those who participated in those programs—myself included. As you can imagine, everyone from formerly incarcerated individuals (whose lives Tommy influenced in some form or fashion) to political figures sang Tommy's praises during the *Governor's Council* hearing. However, there was two members of the *Governor's Council* who openly stated that they did not believe Tommy's story—one of which who seemed to be interrogating Tommy which eventually appeared to be a flat out attack (from questioning Tommy's character and integrity to trying to confuse Tommy and trip him up in his story). Watching this whole exchange, I could see that Tommy was tired (from this all-day event), even confused at times—looking like a *"punch drunk"* boxer after a few rounds with *Muhammad Ali*. After the hearing, Tommy was sent back to the prison. As the enemy (the devil) would do his best to attack Tommy's mind with fear and doubt, God gave me a specific rhema Word with five specific details to tell Tommy to comfort him and let Him know what God had done, was doing, and was about to do in Tommy's behalf.

> *"...God gave me a specific rhema Word with five specific details to tell Tommy to comfort him and let Him know what God had done, was doing, and was about to do in Tommy's behalf."*

The five details were as follows: 1.) *You are coming home* (God is releasing you from prison), 2.) *There's nothing you could do to mess this up*; it's already done (this miracle is not based on your level of faith or doubt; it is based on God's promise to you), 3.) *You will receive a unanimous vote from all eight of the members of the Governor's Council* (they all will agree on the decision to release you—all 8 of them), 4.) *The reason why God allowed you to be attacked so severely during the hearing by one of the Governor's Council members* (who publicly stated that he believed you were lying) *is because God wants you to know, without a shadow of a doubt, that it is Him (God) who is getting you out of prison—and not your 30 years of work, helping people* (God didn't want Tommy to become prideful—thinking that it was his own good works that got him released and, as a result, not give God the glory for keeping His promise and setting Tommy free), 5.) *God is going to expedite your release* (once the decision is announced, you'll be home in April).

I, in my flesh (my own thinking—not God), added a 6th detail, "you will be home by my birthday April 12th, so we can celebrate together. Unfortunately, Tommy came out after my birthday on April 19th (perfect example of man's limitations—God tells man what to do; man does not tell God what to do).

All in all, all five details came to pass. For me, it was easy: God told me to give Tommy a message, so I did—with absolute confidence and no hesitation. Thinking back—even now while I am writing this very sentence (on 12/18/23)—it was almost two years ago when I gave

Tommy that prophetic Word, and Tommy had shared with me that his spirit received that Word immediately. *"I needed that word,"* he said *"to quiet the enemies attacks on my mind."* Tommy shared with me that it was such a timely *Word* that gave him the peace he needed to get him through those final hours of his incarceration. Quite a difference, I would say, from the time—almost 15 years ago—when I told him that I heard from God regarding my own release. I would even go as far as to say that Tommy was able to believe and have the faith necessary to receive this *rhema/prophetic Word* because he had me and other faith-filled Christians in his life (his environment) who were willing to have radical faith to believe in the impossible. Tommy would often tell me that he believed that I had the *gift of faith*. I would simply say that anyone in their right mind would believe it, if they knew God said it.

> *"Someone might say that it was bold, risky, and/or dangerous; I would say that I am glad that I did not try to think/reason it out."*

Today, I ask myself, "Nick, how do you tell a man, your friend and brother, who has been in prison for 30 years—with multiple failed attempts at motions and appeals to both the Superior Court and the Governor's Office—that he is going to be released, now, and there is nothing that he could do to mess this up?" More Specifically, how do you tell a man—in the above-mentioned situation—that he will receive unanimous votes from all eight members of the Governor's Council, when only four votes were needed, and two of the members had publicly stated that they did not believe his story? Furthermore, how do you tell a man "don't worry about how bad the hearing appeared towards the end, it was just a smoke show that God allowed to make sure that you give Him all the glory—and by the way, you'll be out in a few months?" Someone might say that it was bold, risky, and/or dangerous; I would say that I am glad that I did not try to think/reason it out. God told me what to say, and I said it—as soon as Tommy called me the following day after the hearing. Had I had thought about it and try to reason it out, I may have gotten scared and doubted what God had told me. However, what I actually did when God spoke to my spirit was immediately spoke it out loud to another Christian brother. At that point, I was able to hear myself say it out loud with another Christian brother present. At that point, I could not go back on what I had heard in my spirit, which simply made it easier to release when Tommy called me on the phone.

Faith like this—and being sensitive enough to hear the voice of God in such detail—did not just come overnight. It started in my teens and really started to develop in my early 20s spending countless hours with God in prayer, reading His Word (the Bible) fasting, worshiping, and seeking his face. So, during the last couple of years of my incarceration, when this lingering sense of urgency began to increase, God began letting me know that His desire for me was more than just spiritual growth and development; He wanted me to grow and develop in the natural realm, as well, because his desire is that a man walk in wholeness—*not lacking anything* (James 1:4).

As a result, I went from spending almost 7 days a week in the prison church to only spending 2 or 3 days a week in the prison church. I was on a very strict, God ordained, regiment. I had always kept a job (despite the fact that I could not earn *good time);* I was taking college classes with *Boston University*, I was mentoring grown men and *"at-risk"* youth in a program called *2nd Thoughts, Inc.;* I served in the church and in the *Young Men's Ministry* of the church, and I had a serious workout routine that I was committed to. God was stretching my capacity while using programs, organizations, and the people involved to help develop me. Remember, before getting arrested at the age of 22, all I had known was drugs, guns, violence, and crime. I remember Christian brothers in the church approaching me saying that they were "worried" about me because they had not seen me in church much. To them, going to church 2 to 3 times a week was not enough—and it meant that I was struggling spiritually. I tried to explain to them that I was going to be released soon, and that God was preparing me for the outside world. But their religious mindsets that were stuck on the one scripture *"seek first the kingdom of God and His righteousness"* (Matthew 6:33 NKJV) did not have the capacity to incorporate other scriptures that state, *"if anyone does not provide for his own, and especially for those of his household, he has denied the faith and is worse than an unbeliever"* (1 Timothy 5:8 NKJV)—and *"anyone who has been stealing must steal no longer, but must work, doing something useful with their own hands, that they may have something to share with those in need"* (Ephesians 4:28 NIV). So, in their eyes, if they did not see me in the church about 5 to 7 times a week, it meant that I was struggling spiritually. I, on the other hand, understood that God was working on me. I understood that keeping a job was building character, integrity, and work ethic. I understood that getting an education would also contribute to me being able to provide for my family.

> *"I, on the other hand, understood that God was working on me."*

I understood that being healthy and staying fit would expand my years on earth—which, in turn, would increase my impact on the world. I understood that mentoring men and *"at-risk"* youth was also God's work. Overall, I understood that God was expanding my capacity, developing my character, and teaching me how to balance life— wearing multiple hats because life would require me to wear multiple hats upon my release—as a child of God, husband, father, provider, leader, etc. God was teaching me that I needed Him to be successful in all that I did, and that I needed to invite him into every aspect of my life—not just the time I spent in church. Yes, this book is about the *"**Absolute Severity of Environment**"* and one of those *absolute severities* is that God remains in your environment at all times—wherever you go—and in regard to whatever you do.

CHAPTER 7

RE-POTTED BACK INTO SOCIETY

*"Perfume and incense bring joy to the heart,
and the pleasantness of a friend
springs from their heartfelt advice."*
(Proverbs 27:9 NIV)

"Being re-potted back into society is like the plant that was re-potted in the forest."

The Release From Prison

Being re-potted back into society is like the plant that was re-potted in the forest. Just as the forest had the greatest natural ingredients of nature's soil with plenty of space for roots to grow strong, deep, and wide—creating a solid foundation for optimal growth—so also did society provide the greatest potential for growth. I remember it vividly. I was laying on a mattress in a prison cell on the second floor of building 1-3 in *MCI Norfolk* prison. Every appeal that I submitted to the courts to overturn my convictions was denied. Every motion that I had petitioned to the courts was denied. And at this point, I had exhausted every legal opportunity to get out of prison. I remember experiencing so much pain, thinking about my children growing up without me, and simply realizing that prison was not for me. I remember the pain that I was experiencing in my soul being so bad that I could taste it. I could literally taste pain in my mouth. I remember crying out to God and telling Him that I could not handle this pain, and that I did not have any more capacity to stay in this prison any longer. Yes, God had told me some time towards the beginning of my incarceration that I was not going to do 15 years in prison. What He did not tell me was, how long I would actually do. And this cry was my final cry to cash in on His promise. I do not remember, exactly, if it was a day later, a week later, or a month later—when my study partner (Luis)—stood outside my cell window yelling my name, "Yo Nick, Yo Nick." I went to the window, and there he was telling me about a new decision that had just passed in the *Supreme Judicial Court*, regarding the *Melendez Diaz* case and the *George Vazquez* case. The first thing I did was to bring the information to an *"inmate attorney"* named Jim. (Note to self: when you are on a *desperate pursuit for growth*—making the control of your environment a top priority, both internally and externally, associating with intellectuals will become a normal aspect of life. In the beginning of your *desperate pursuit for growth*, you will have to identify them and choose them intentionally. As you grow—and start to realize your growth and worth—eventually, you will start to attract them (other intellectuals). Furthermore, both groups (the *chosen intellectuals* and *attracted intellectuals*) are ordained by God—some for a season and some for a lifetime. Remember, God promises to place people in our lives to bless us—in some way, shape, or form. As you remain committed to your *desperate pursuit for growth*, over time, you will notice that the majority (if not all) of your associates are intellectuals—seasoned and experienced individuals in their fields—with everyone having something to contribute to another. At this point, you will be experiencing what the *Bible* refers to as *"iron sharpening iron"* (Proverbs 27:17). However, the desire for growth and gain should not be one's only desire, but simply the *"why"* behind making someone else's life—if not the world—better. The dangerous question for many is the *when*. When, in one's *desperate pursuit for growth,* is he or she safe enough to reach back and help another—without being pulled back into what they desperately fought so hard to get out of? The answer to this will be addressed in the last *part* of this book—when one truly becomes a *Master Farmer/Gardener.*

> *"However, the desire for growth and gain should not be one's only desire, but simply the "why" behind making someone else's life—if not the world— better."*

Jim was a gentleman who was a few years older than myself and was serving time in the same unit as me. We had become cool over the years when he had asked me to draw up a workout regimen for himself because he had hit a plateau in the gym. I informed him about the *Melendez Diaz* and *George Vasquez* cases that had been ruled upon in the *Supreme Judicial Court,* and I had given him the details of my case, so he could do some research to determine if the two cases pertained to my case. After about a day or two, Jim got back to me saying that the two cases that were ruled upon in the *SJC* had everything to do with my case, and he suggested that I contact my attorney immediately—and that is exactly what I did. My attorney informed me that although the two cases that were ruled upon in the *SJC* did, in fact, pertain to my case, there was no guarantee that the courts would release me soon or even at all. And I knew what she was saying was accurate because I could see it on the inside of the facility. Some individuals who had 15+ year— *minimum mandatory*—prison sentences (for drug trafficking) were being released. One individual—who I knew—was given a high bail, and his family was able to gather up the money and bail him out. Whereas, other individuals, despite their cases being overturned, were still held in prison without bail—or were given such a high bail that they (nor anyone they knew) could afford it. So my attorney explained to me that she was going to have to file two motions in *superior court* (and go before the same judge who sentenced me) arguing that (Motion # 1) the *Melendez Diaz* and *George Vazquez* cases that were ruled upon in the *Supreme Judicial Court* did, in fact, pertain to my case; therefore, the courts should overturn my conviction—and that (Motion # 2) releasing me was a good idea.

My attorney already had everything that she needed for motion # 1 because all of the arguments regarding the *Melendez Diaz* and *George Vasquez* cases were already argued in the *Supreme Judicial Court*, and the *SJC* already ruled in favor of both of those cases. The *Supreme Judicial Court* is a higher court than the *Worcester Superior Court* that I was indicted, tried, and convicted in, so my attorney did not have to re-argue those cases—she only had to show that the chemist, who tested the drugs in my case, did not, in fact, show up and/or testify in my trial, which was easy because every witness in the trial was documented.

"As you can imagine—all and only by the Grace of God—I was accepted, and a six-member group was assigned to me."

Regarding motion # 2, most of the work was also completed and ready for argument. I had kept my nose clean, for the most part, throughout my incarceration, I was heavily involved in the church and *Young Men's Ministry*, I was mentoring men and *"at risk"* youth in *2nd Thoughts Inc.*, I had kept a job throughout the entirety of my sentence, and I had completed two years of college with Boston University (with a GPA of 3.5.). In addition, while attending *Boston University*, I had signed up for a program called *Partakers: College Behind Bars* which is an educational mentoring program for Boston University students who are incarcerated. However, this program is not for all incarcerated students. Students had to write an essay explaining why they thought they should be assigned a group of mentors. Lots of people applied for this program but not everyone got accepted. As you can imagine—all and only by the Grace of God—I was accepted, and a six-member group was assigned to me. Again, God promises to put people in our lives to bless us. In this group were an engineer, judge, psychologist, politician, and two college professors. I did not know that Christy was a judge until she told me after my release. Collectively, they decided to only inform me that Christy had a degree in law from Harvard. They did not think it was a good idea for other inmates to know that a judge was coming up to visit me. I did not receive much, if any, educational mentoring because I wanted to see if I could handle college on my own. However, I did, in fact, enjoy the visits because no one from my family was visiting me since they were all felons, and did not try to go through the extensive process of appeal considering that they were immediate family and could have obtained special permission to visit me. My *Partakers* team and I became very close over the last two years of my incarceration.

> *"She said, 'it will most likely be several months before we receive a ruling,' and I responded, 'my God can do anything.'"*

They would come up to visit me two at a time which meant that I got visits almost every week for the last two years of my sentence. They were a part of the small handful of individuals who I would tell that I was going to be released soon, and yes, they too looked at me like I was crazy—knowing that I had a 15-to-17-year prison sentence with 15 of those years being a *minimum mandatory sentence*. However, when the time came for my case to be brought back into court, they all stepped up to the plate faithfully, and wrote letters of recommendation and even showed up to the hearing. On the day of the hearing, right before going into court, I asked my attorney how long a decision/ruling would typically take for this type of case. She said, "it will most likely be several months before we receive a ruling," and I responded, "*my God can do anything.*" We entered the court room, and I was instructed to have a seat. The judge introduced himself and instructed my attorney to proceed with the motions that she had filed before the courts. My attorney pointed out that the chemist who tested the drugs in my case never showed up to my trial and/or testified under oath— which meant that the new laws passed in the *Supreme Judicial Court* concerning the *Melendez Diaz* and *George Vasquez* cases applied to my case, and the *Superior Court* had to overturn my conviction. She then did her best to sing my praises regarding the above-mentioned accomplishments and behavior while incarcerated.

Next the prosecution began to argue her case. There was not much that she could say regarding whether or not the *Melendez Diaz* and *George Vasquez* cases pertain to my case because it was pretty clear cut, but she did, however, pull out the heavy arsenal regarding my criminal record and life of crime which led to my conviction and 15-to-17-year prison sentence. I mean this woman "*went in.*" She did her research and tore me to shreds. When she was finished, I almost believed that I should not be released from prison. She called me a *menace to society* and pointed out the fact that from 1988 (my first charge at the age of 8 years old) all the way up until the beginning of 2003, there was not a single year in which I did not commit new crimes and pick up new criminal charges.

Then, the judge spoke, *"I believe Nickolas has changed. When people like this show up in his behalf and put their names and reputations on the line, I believe he has changed. I remember the young man who stood before me eight years ago, and it is not the man who stands before me today, so I am releasing him."* My heart jumped, and I took an unintentional and rapid deep breath—as if my lungs and heart jumped simultaneously—as tears immediately filled my eyes. Because of the seriousness of the crime, the judge stated that I would be given an ankle bracelet to wear. It was a Friday, so he ordered those involved to have my ankle bracelet ready by Monday, and he told me that I would have to go back to the prison for the weekend. It was music to my ears. I was being released. After 8 years of incarceration. God had honored His Word, fulfilled His promise, and made sure that I did not do 15 years in prison—just as He had said.

Please pay attention to how God works. Two cases that I had known nothing about were being fought—behind the scenes—for several years. A law that had specifically applied to my case had just appeared out of thin air, and God had given me back seven years of my life. Although I was released from prison, the reversal of my convictions did not mean that I was innocent. It simply meant that I had to fight the case all over again—from the beginning. After six months of going in and out of court, the *District Attorney's Office* said that they no longer wanted to prosecute the case. When we inquired about the reason why, they stated that they could no longer find any of the drugs, gun and over 300 rounds of ammunition— apparently, they had mysteriously vanished. TO GOD BE ALL THE GLORY!

> *"However, I was fully aware of the fact that I had to leave my hometown —Worcester Massachusetts—and start afresh."*

Leaving Home—Uncharted Waters

I was released from the *Worcester District Court House* in *Worcester, Massachusetts,* in the month of November in the year of 2010 (3 Days Before Thanksgiving). The courts approved my release upon the restrictions of an *ankle bracelet* (home arrest) to be carried out at my grandmother's house. However, I was fully aware of the fact that I had to leave my hometown—*Worcester Massachusetts*—and start afresh. I knew that *"bad company corrupts good character,"* and despite the fact that I had worked so hard over the years— working on my character— it could be corrupted, if surrounded by the wrong environment. You see, my father, mother, brothers and sister still lived in *Worcester,* and they still were heavily involved in reckless living—drinking, drugging, and committing crimes.   Therefore, it was an *ABSOLUTE* necessity to leave Worcester. Furthermore, leaving Worcester was so essential and so crucial for myself that I left with two suitcases, filled with *second-hand clothes* (used clothes that was given to me), and went straight into a homeless shelter in *Boston, Massachusetts—Pilgram Congregational Church* on Columbia Road. I was surrounded by individuals who were intoxicated by drugs and alcohol, smelled extremely disgusting, and were rude and defiant. The homeless shelter itself was nasty, smelled disgusting, and was not well managed to say the least. *But God,* however, granted me favor in the eyes of the Director of the homeless shelter. The Director gave me a room upstairs, entirely for myself. While approximately 100 men shared a single open space, I, on the other hand, had a room all to myself. In addition, this Director, by the name of *Joe Texeira* was also the Director of a *Career Development Program* called *MAP* (*Moving Ahead Program*). After interviewing me during the application process for the homeless shelter, he said, "you know what? A spot just opened up in the *MAP* program, and I would love to get you into this program right away." A female had gotten kicked out because she had tested positive for drugs. There were people who waited 4 to 6 months (or longer) to get into the *MAP* program, and God had opened the door for me the very first night I stepped into the homeless shelter. Again, *TO GOD BE ALL THE GLORY!*

This program got me into an apartment, paid my rent for the first four months, taught me basic computer skills and how to write a résumé. This was specifically important for myself because when I went into jail at the age of 22, text messaging had just been created, and I had never sent a text message or email in my entire life. In addition, the program trained individuals on job interviewing strategies and provided video recorded *mock-interviews* that allowed an individual to see his or herself on video, evaluate his or her strengths and weaknesses, and make the appropriate corrections to their job interviewing practices. The program had an additional feature called *Studio Shine* in which they provided professional clothes for individuals who were going on job interviews—and the clothes (from head to toe) were free. The program also assisted individuals in applying for *Welfare, SSI, Section 8 Housing*, and regular housing. While loving this new environment of learning, two more amazing things happened to me: I had gotten back into school— *Boston University*—and had gotten myself a job.

The Denial and Approval

Initially, when I had applied for financial aid to get back into school, I was denied because I had never filed for *Selective Services* between the ages of 18 and 26. *Selective Services* was a federal requirement put in place so that the government could draft you for war if they wanted to—Army, Navy, Military, for example. I remember being 18 years old when I received that piece of paper in the mail back in 1998. I was a young punk who was selling drugs and living the street life as previously mentioned earlier in this book. I remember receiving the letter to file for *Selective Services* and ripping it up, stating, "I will *never* go fight in the *white man's* war." Well, with every action, there is a reaction, and the reaction of that decision meant that I could not receive any federal funding— including financial aid for a college education. I was devastated. I had attended college (part-time) for the last four years of my incarceration— which meant that I had only completed two years of college (my freshman and sophomore years). It was bad enough that the *four-year scholarship* that I had earned by testing into *Boston University* was stripped from me the moment I was released—and to make matters worse, I was being denied financial aid.

> *"I remember receiving the letter to file for Selective Services and ripping it up, stating, 'I will never go fight in the white man's war'."*

Financially, I could not afford to take care of myself, so I certainly could not afford to pay for my own education—specifically, at *Boston University*. Moreover, people who were not used to God doing the miraculous in their own lives started talking to me about settling for community college and/or online classes, but I refused to listen to them and insisted on getting an education from *Boston University*. The college I started at was going to be the college I finished at; I simply had no idea how I was going to make it happen, or should I say, "I simply had no idea how God was going to make it happen." In my own efforts, I reached out to financial aid, requesting some type of appeal. The woman, very gladly and confidently, said, "*Absolutely, I will send you appeal documents to fill out; however, I have been doing this job for over 20 years, and not once has a single appeal—for individuals who have failed to file for Selective Services between the ages of 18 and 26–been approved.*" I can fake it like I had all the *faith* in the world, but—to be completely honest with you—her comment let almost all of the air out of my *faith balloon*. Like the man in Mark 9:14-29, this was a moment to say, "*Lord, I believe, but help my unbelief.*" Then, I called my godmother Christy. She was one of the educational mentors with *Partakers* who I mentioned earlier—the judge. In fact, this may have been the moment in which she/we placed a name on our relationship—my *"unofficial godmother"* (her words). Not exactly sure why she added the word *"unofficial."* Maybe it was because she does not believe in God (my hope and prayer is that she will by the end of this book—and if you are a believer, you can pray in agreement with me for her Salvation as well) and/or maybe because she was not there in church with me to dedicate me (as a baby) to God as official godparents would do. Nonetheless, I called my *unofficial godmother*, who I will refer to throughout the remainder of this book as my "godmother." Her name is *Christina Harms*—who is now a retired probate court judge after 23 years—and she was one of the six members of the team that was assigned to me by the *Partakers: College Behind Bars* program. I had only been free from incarceration for a few months, and we—my godmother and I—had not seen each other in a little while, so she recommended that we go out and have lunch, so we could catch up and she could check in on my progress as a *newly law-abiding citizen.*

> *"At lunch, I fought to hold back tears as I explained to her that I had to be back in school."*

At lunch, I fought to hold back tears as I explained to her that I had to be back in school. I explained— to the best of my ability—that I was used to a certain structure and that school was a part of that structure. I explained how being a part of something and working towards something that was bigger than myself was extremely essential and crucial for my survival in the *"real world,"* and how not being in school meant *death* to someone like me. You, as the reader, are probably thinking to yourself, *"this kid Nick is pretty extreme."* However, that is exactly how I felt at the moment—coming from the family, household, and environment that I had come from, and then being released from prison at the age of 30. Moreover, my godmother just sat there, enjoying her lunch, not really moved at all by all my emotion. Then, when I was finished pouring my heart out, she—very simply and very plainly— said, "don't worry about it, everything will be fine." I remember thinking to myself, "did she hear anything I just said?" Not only did I pour out my heart and point out all of my fears, but I had also explained to her how the woman at *financial aid* had assured me of the fact that after 20+ years of her working in that department, not a single appeal concerning failure to file for *Selective Services* had been approved. So, looking at my godmother's calm (and *not-moved-at-all)* facial expression, I had to ask, "did you not hear what I said?" And she, very calmly, said, "I did, now eat your food before it gets cold." Long story short, my godmother contacted them, drew up my appeal herself, and the same woman who told me that my appeal would be denied, called my cell phone to inform me that everything regarding my financial aid had been situated, and that all she needed me to do was sign a few documents. To God Be All The Glory. God is funny in this way—He will use the same person who told you "no," to tell you "yes." He will use the same person who closed the door on you to open the door for you. He will use the same person who slandered you, betrayed you, abandoned you, and hurt you to be the same person who defends you, rescues you, invites you, and promotes you. Just like in the story of blind Bartimaeus, when he cried out to Jesus, the same people who rebuked Bartimaeus and told him to be quiet— were the same people who Jesus commanded to bring Bartimaeus to Him, so He could restore his sight (Mark 10:46-52).

> *"I showed up early and left late every single day."*

From Almost Fired To Promoted

By the grace of God and the skills acquired by learning from Boston University, the *MAP* program, and other professionals (regarding résumé writing, and job interviewing skills)— I landed my first legitimate job working for the business department at the *Salvation Army Ray and Joan Kroc Corps Community Center* in Boston Massachusetts. Although I was honest with the interviewer regarding having a criminal record, I did not know—at the time—that the *higher-ups* only approved my employment because they had not obtained and/or viewed my criminal record. It was somehow lost or misplaced. I, on the other hand, was so excited to have my first legitimate job (upon my release from prison)—not doing manual labor but being able to wear shoes and slacks—at this newly built $50 million facility. I was fortunate enough to have been hired before their *soft opening* and *grand opening* in which the mayor, several news outlets, and *Paul Pierce* from the *Boston Celtics* had attended. This facility was the talk of the town and the hope of the city. The chaos of all its moving parts was such a beautiful thing to be a part of. Being hired at $11 an hour was such an upgrade from scrubbing toilets in prison for $1.00 per day, so I worked as much as I could. When people called out of work or left early, I always offered my help to assist. There was always a need for help in every department, so I offered my help in every department. I showed up early and left late every single day. I had heard an older gentleman once say, *"if you are on time, you are late, and if you are early, you are on time,"* so I adopted the principal as my own. I would show up to work a half hour before scheduled. One time, I was involved in a car accident on my way to work and still made it to work early. Being self-disciplined with time meant a lot to me due to the fact that I had grown up in a household that displayed no self-discipline. I loved the $11 an hour pay (in comparison to prison pay), and I loved learning new things.

> *"All in all, I did this several times with several different managers— maxing out my overtime, learning multiple departments, and knowing that I was contributing to a cause much bigger than myself."*

Although I was given a *part-time* position, I was going home with *full-time* and *overtime* pay. I loved being a part of something bigger than myself, and I truly wanted the facility to succeed on all fronts. The place was amazing. It had an indoor water park, an official NCAA, basketball court, state of the art work-out/fitness areas, indoor rock climbing, educational and afterschool programs for kids, a daycare, a nursery, a culinary arts program, church, and so much more. The success of this facility meant the success of our community— not to mention the fact that it helped keep kids like myself off the streets in some of the roughest neighborhoods in Boston. I put in so many hours without noticing it that management approached me and said, "Nick, we love your help, and we really need it, but legally we can only allow you to work so many hours." I remember, specifically, during a major event in which the facility was understaffed— management had reminded me to punch out because I would exceed the approvable hours for the week. When I asked the manager how she was going to handle the rest of the event and cleanup, she responded by stating that she would have to stay longer until the work was complete. So, I went to the *punch clock* and punched out and came back and helped her until everything was completed. At the end of the evening, she voiced how much she appreciated my help— stating that she could have never done it without me—and I told her that it was my pleasure, and to never hesitate to ask if she ever needed my assistance again. All in all, I did this several times with several different managers—maxing out my overtime, learning multiple departments, and knowing that I was contributing to a cause much bigger than myself. A few weeks later, HR—in New York—eventually found my criminal record, and sent a woman from the HR department in *Canton, Massachusetts* down to meet with me. Before our meeting, she had touched base with all of the managers who I had worked with, and she had concluded that there simply had to be a mistake. She did not believe that the person she was reading about, via the criminal record, was the same person who all of these managers were giving glowing comments and feedback about. She legitimately thought it was a mistake—maybe a person with a similar name and/or Social Security number. After sitting me down and explaining this to me, she said that we had to go over the details in the CORI that was before her. It took her about five minutes to go over my first criminal charge in 1988 when I was eight years old— "breaking and entering." I said, "yes, ma'am that was me."

"'That is who I used to be,' I said, 'young and stupid, but this is who I am today...'"

As she started to go over the second crime on my criminal record, I knew that we would be there all day because I have a criminal record longer than *Blue Hill Avenue*. So, I kindly interrupted her. "Ma'am," I said, "with all due respect, everything in that criminal record is me. Yes, I did it all." She looked at me in shock. "That is who I used to be," I said, "young and stupid, but this is who I am today—a man who works hard at his job, currently in the process of graduating from a career development program, and attending *Boston University* with goals and dreams to live a better life." Then, while handing me her business card, she said, "unfortunately, we are most likely going to have to let you go. As you know, we have a lot of children who utilize this facility." Again, I said, "ma'am, with all due respect, not one of my crimes involve children." She said, "I understand; I'm just trying to give you a heads up," as she extended her hand that was holding her business card. I was upset but did my best to hide it. I almost turned around and walked away without grabbing her business card, but I swallowed my pride— and my anger— mustered up a half smile, reached out and grabbed her card and said, "I understand; you have a blessed day." Not knowing what to do, I called my godmother Christy. She and a few others started making phone calls and sending emails, once again, putting their names and reputations on the line in my behalf—promising that if my employer decided to keep me, it would be a decision they would not regret. A couple of weeks later, I was called back into the office with the CEO—and the same HR lady from *Canton*—and was told that they had made their decision which was to continue with my employment. I was extremely grateful and excited. Shortly after, when upper management decided to create a new department, it was asked in a board meeting—"who should we choose to run this department?" In that board meeting sat all of the managers who I had previously worked with and learned from, and unanimously (and some simultaneously) all agreed and stated, "Nick can do it." At that point, I was promoted, and individuals who had previously served as my superiors, I was then given the responsibility of being their superior. Furthermore, when the Salvation Army threw their first, ever, nationwide business trip, they chose four people out of 120 employees, and who do you think was one of the four? That's right— it was I. There I was, all expenses paid, in a luxurious hotel, learning business—who would have thought? From the prison cell to the boardroom. TO GOD BE ALL THE GLORY!

> *"After graduating the MAP program, I had no idea where I was going to live. The four months of paid rent had come to an end, and I had to figure something out—so I thought."*

First Year Out

After graduating from the *MAP* program, I had no idea where I was going to live. The four months of paid rent had come to an end, and I had to figure something out—so I thought. My mentors from *Partakers: College Behind Bars* were so determined to make sure that I did not fail, the six of them had come up with a plan to allow me to live with each one of them for six months at a time, until I got on my feet. Talk about the Glory of God. *Jehovah Jireh* means, *The God Who Provides*. The first person I was scheduled to live with was Linda—in her huge and beautiful home in Newton, Massachusetts— outside of Boston. Linda's two kids were off to college/professionalism, while Linda and her husband, Tom— both retired engineers— enjoyed retirement, and some of the other finer things in life. For approximately six months, I stayed with Linda and Tom at their home, in a guest room, while working full-time at the Salvation Army and working towards finishing my degree at *Boston University*. It was during those six months that I had obtained my first vehicle (upon release from prison), and had decided that it was time for me to get my own apartment. With plans on reuniting with *Crystal* and my boys, I had to get a three-bedroom apartment, and it *"just had to be"* in Newton because I had learned that Newton was ranked like fourth in all of America for best public schools. As crazy as this all sounded to my godmother, Christy—a judge living in Wellesley Massachusetts (also a well-off town)—having to listen to a kid from the hood, fresh out of prison, saying that he *"has to"* live in Newton—she did everything in her power to help me get it done. By the *Grace of God*, and within the first year of my release, I had moved into a homeless shelter in Boston with two suitcases of *"hand me down"* clothes, graduated from a career development program (*MAP*), got back into school—*Boston University*—obtained a job, received a major promotion, got my first vehicle (an SUV), an apartment in Newton, and a brand new, lime green, *Kawasaki Ninja* that I had always wanted.

> *"During the eight years of my incarceration, there was nothing that I wanted more than to be reunited with Crystal and my sons."*

By the second year of my release, I started my first business after attending the *"2012 Man-Power Conference"* hosted by *TD Jakes* at *"The Potters House"* in Dallas Texas— a business that I am proud of and thankful for, and still currently own while writing this book, to-day—nearly 12 years later. The *"new to me"* environment of society—and its nutrition—was producing growth from *sub-environments* like Church, *MAP*, *Boston University*, the work field, and the *"real world."* However, remember, the re-potting process into larger and more nutritious environments, also involve/include more exposure and more danger.

> *"The pieces to the puzzle of the dream that I had dreamt of—for eight years in prison—were finally starting to come together. UNTIL..."*

The Fall

During the eight years of my incarceration, there was nothing that I wanted more than to be reunited with Crystal and my sons. More specifically, the 8 years of little to no communication between Crystal and I, also forced me to wrap my head around the possibility of her moving on and possibly being in a relationship with someone else. I never viewed Crystal as a fast *"hood-rat chick"* who slept around with multiple men, so my thoughts were, *"If she has been with another man, he must be a good man with plans to do right by her and our children."* Yes, in my confidence, I also thought, *"Good man or not, he has nothing on me."* More importantly, three days after my release, on Thanksgiving day, I received a phone call from my sons who I had not spoken to in almost 8 years. I also spoke to Crystal for the first time in almost 8 years as well, and for the first two years of my release, we talked on the phone, worked on our marriage, and took flights back-and-forth from Boston to Vegas to spend time together. After helping Crystal pay off all of her bills in the West Coast, we packed up all of their belongings— into shipping containers— and sent it all to Boston, where it would meet us after our flight with the kids—*Pito* and *Niko*. With things looking like they were finally starting to fall into place— there was something that was weighing on my soul heavily and had been doing so for many years: the situation regarding *Nick Jr.* The name of *Nick Jr.'s* mother is Monique. I did not find out that Nick Jr. was my son until he was eight months old (in the year "2000"), and after I had been dating Crystal for several months. When I met Crystal, in the beginning of 2000, she had just moved to Worcester with Pito, who was two years old at the time. Eventually, *Nick Jr.* would end up living with myself, Crystal and Pito; then, Niko was born in November of 2001. When I went away to prison, in the beginning of 2003, my sons ages were 5,3, and 1– Pito was 5, Nick Jr. was 3, and Niko was 1. After approximately 8 months (after my arrest), Crystal was forced to move back in with her mother who (at the time) had lived out in California—from Boston it is literally the opposite side of the country. Crystal's mother had determined that it was already a huge responsibility to take in Crystal, Pito, and Niko, so

Nick Jr., who was not her biological grandson, could not go with them all to California. Because I was in prison and Monique was too busy living the fast life (drinking, drugging, and partying)—and because neither one of us (Monique and I) had family members who were not also drinking, drugging, and partying—Nick Jr. ended up in foster care. Nick Jr. was three years old when I was sentenced to 15 to 17 years in prison, and he was 11 years old when I got released. Then, after two years of being released back into society—while spending those two years working on my marriage with Crystal and fighting a custody battle for Nick Jr., he was 13 years old. The pieces to the puzzle of the dream that I had dreamt of—for eight years in prison—were finally starting to come together. UNTIL...

You—as the reader—are probably wondering, "until what?"

Until, I lost the custody trial for my son, Nick Jr., in which he was adopted by two white homosexual men—while simultaneously finding out that Crystal was still keeping in touch with a young man from her past during the two years we were working on our marriage.

The blow that the championship boxer did not see coming, came in a three blow combination that knocked him down—Nick Jr.'s adoption, the affair, and the poor decision to try to slightly numb the pain and block out the confusion with alcohol. This three-punch combo initiated *"the fall."*

"One of the first mistakes that I made was thinking that I was going to use alcohol to slightly numb the pain and keep myself distracted."

Let's keep this simple and not make this more complicated than necessary. If you were in a car accident or had some kind of physical injury, the best environment to be in would be a hospital. If you broke your tooth, had a toothache, or an oral infection, the best environment to be in would be a dentist. If your vehicle was leaking fluid or making some weird noise or smell, or had warning lights blinking in the dashboard, the best environment to be in would be at the auto shop with a mechanic. Although I did not have a physical injury, an oral emergency, or a vehicle issue, there was an environment that I could have found and/or created that would have provided protection, nutritional provision, healing, and new growth. One of the first mistakes that I made was thinking that I was going to use alcohol to slightly numb the pain and keep myself distracted. In all reality, I knew better. Alcohol had always been my drug of choice. In addition, I am half white and half black, and my Irish side of the family all drink like fish, and my African-American side of the family all drink like fish. So, no matter how you explain and/or understand it, it was a poor decision. Like they say, "the apple does not fall far from the tree." Some can relate to generational curses. Others, understand and trust science more particularly— knowing that addiction itself is hereditary and genetically transferred from one generation to the next.

"This lonely void only increased and had me looking for family, friends, relationships, and intimacy in all of the wrong places."

They understand that when a newborn's parents are addicted to drugs and/or alcohol— more specifically, during conception and/or pregnancy—the child's likelihood of being prone to addiction is significantly increased. This has to do with the cortex of the brain. In other words, the addictive behavior/condition of the parents will determine how thin or thick the child's brain-cortex will be— which determines how much the child will be prone to addiction. Like I said, "I knew better." It was simply a poor decision— and that decision kept me in environments that provided and/or served alcohol. Which, in turn, kept me in environments where others were drinking also (misery loves company). And these types of environments support and encourage drinking. Not to mention, all of the pain and confusion that I was experiencing that kept me feeling alone, despite how many people I surround myself with. These overwhelming feelings of loneliness drew me back to my hometown, to what was familiar (like a pig in the mud). This lonely void only increased and had me looking for family, friends, relationships, and intimacy in all of the wrong places. Being around old friends who betrayed me and family members who stab me in the back just to feel a sense of belonging was doing more damage than damage control. Most of my family members and old friends were still doing the same things they were doing 10 years ago—drinking, drugging, partying, going from one dead end job to the next (or having no job at all), no plan, no hope, no action. When you put on some nice clothes, try to look good and smell good, and are surrounded by a room full of others who are drinking and smoking—for the moment—you do not look like what you are going through. Everyone is laughing, everyone is drinking, and you do not look like the person who is trying to numb their pain and distract their mind. It was clear to me that the people I was surrounding myself with— despite the fact that they were family, friends, and familiar—they were also all worse off than myself. And— as sick as this sounds—sometimes being around people who were worse off than myself made me slightly feel better about myself, situation, and condition. But more importantly, I was the only person in the room who knew that I was better than this. One might think to him or her self that knowing he or she is *better than this* is everything one would need to pick them self up and dust them self off— unfortunately, for myself, it was not enough. So I continued to wallow in familiar, negative, toxic, non-nutritional environments for approximately five years—stuck— not healing the way that I should have been, not learning the way that I should have been, not developing the way that I should have been, not building the way that I should have been, not growing the way that I should have been, not producing and being fruitful the way I should have been, not protecting the way that I should have been, not providing the way that I should have been, not leading the way that I should have been, and not serving the way I should have been—stuck.

> *"Before I dive into escaping the grip of death and being delivered from strongholds that could have taken my life (and almost did on numerous occasions)..."*

Before I dive into escaping the grip of death and being delivered from strongholds that could have taken my life (and almost did on numerous occasions), I would like us to think about the already existing environments that I could have sought out for assistance, information, motivation, inspiration, healing, positivity, accountability, encouragement, growth and development. Today, as a *"Master Farmer/Gardener"*, I would like us to also think about the *custom* environment that could have been created and utilized to best address what I was going through. In fact, I would like you to take a moment to write these things down. I would like you to momentarily pretend to be my doctor who is prescribing a small list of *environments* that could have made a positive impact on my life versus the familiar environment I chose with alcohol, falling/failing family members and friends. After you create this small list of environments, we are going to compare it with where I actually went (environment) and what I actually did. Then, before the close of this book, you'll get my suggestions as a *"Master Farmer/ Gardener"* regarding how to create your own custom environment that will only lead to your growth, development, and success in every area of your life. One might be asking oneself, "Well, how bad could his alcohol addiction have been? Great question—and an important one. Although addiction is something that takes place internally, there are some external details that could shed some light on how severe the addiction was.

> *"I had told myself that if my parents couldn't do it, and if my grandparents couldn't do it, it was simply something that was going to be with me for the rest of my life."*

For example, years went by without a day of sobriety. I would go to sleep drunk, wake up drunk, and spend every minute of the day intoxicated (for years). More specifically, because liquor stores did not open until 9 AM, I would have to purchase enough alcohol to stay drunk throughout the night and have enough left over in the morning when I woke up around 5 AM or 6 AM because my body could not handle the withdrawal symptoms for the 3 to 4 hours, I would have to wait for a liquor store to become open. They say that the withdrawal symptoms from alcohol can be more dangerous and even deadlier than the withdrawal symptoms of heroin and/or any other opiate. In fact, when a person goes to a medical facility or detox facility for the purpose of detoxing from alcohol (becoming sober), they are fed a medication that slowly helps their body wean off of the alcohol and subside the withdrawal symptoms. The addiction was so bad that I could not simply watch the television—and see someone drinking any type of alcoholic beverage—without, myself, getting up and going to the refrigerator to grab a drink. I could not drive by a liquor store without stopping and making a purchase. And in the neighborhood that I resided in—off of Blue Hill Avenue (and the Mission Hill area)— there was a liquor store on every corner. I remember one summer—I tried to quit. I locked myself in my bedroom, had previously bought several bottles of Gatorade, and had the air conditioner on full blast. Although the room was an icebox, I soaked my bed in sweat—body shaking and in tremendous pain— ultimately, giving up, crossing the street, and purchasing the next bottle of vodka. After several failed attempts to quit drinking over the years, I had come to the *false conclusion* that alcohol was something I would never overcome. I had told myself that if my parents couldn't do it, and if my grandparents couldn't do it, it was simply something that was going to be with me for the rest of my life. I had known that Grandma Nettie had always kept a little stash of brown liquor, and Grandma Chris drank pretty consistently as well. My grandpa Joe died with a 30 pack still in the refrigerator, and *OBD* (my father's father) died as a drinker as well. All my siblings drank, all my cousins drank, and all my aunts and uncles drank as well.

> *"...I poured every drop of alcohol down the kitchen sink and told God that if I died because of this addiction, it was on Him."*

One day, on October 17, 2018 (a Wednesday), I was not only done with alcoholism, but I was done living the life that I was living and simply wanted to end it all. Knowing that my addiction was so bad that my body was dependent upon the alcohol— and knowing that quitting *cold turkey* could have killed me because my organs could have shut down— I poured every drop of alcohol down the kitchen sink and told God that if I died because of this addiction, it was on Him. I told God that I was ready to die— and if my organs shut down, it was His problem and not mine. In my final attempt to *"fall forward"*— a concept that I later learned from a close friend/brother *Alex Green Jr.* who played for the NFL's *New York Jets* and *Green Bay Packers*— I challenged God to show me what He could do with my life if I never had a drink again. I figured, since I was at the end of my rope—and was willing to die— I could at least *fall forward* into the hands of our God. The concept of *falling forward,* in regard to football, points out the fact that in the game and on the field, you are going to take hits and fall in your attempt to gain yards. Because falling is almost inevitable, on every play, a player must make an effort to deliberately fall forward on the field to gain as much yardage as possible. Since my desire was to kill alcoholism, running the risk of killing myself, I was going to make an effort to fall forward into the hands of my Savior—to see if He would let me die— or would He do something else with my life? If there was a possibility of going down, I wanted to go down with God. I told God that I was going to give him my body as a *"living sacrifice,* holy and pleasing to [Him]" (Romans 12:1 NIV) and would completely put "aside the sin that so easily besets us" (Hebrews 12:1 KJV). No more drugs, no more alcohol, no more fornication, no more masturbation, no more pornography, and no more gluttonous eating—I had decided to present my body as a living sacrifice to God, so I could see what He could do in me, for me, and through me—once my temple (mind & body) was clean and clear. My Pastor, *Matthew K Thompson*, once told me that *"anything you starve, has to die."*

PART 3: MASTERING RETENTION & RECIDIVISM PREVENTION BY BECOMING A MASTER FARMER/ GARDENER

FOR SELF AND FUTURE GENERATIONS

CHAPTER 8

ENVIRONMENT HYPERFOCUS

"The way of fools seems right to them,
but the wise listen to advice."
(Proverbs 12:15)

Cleaning & Filling The House
(Internally & Externally)

"When an impure spirit comes out of a person, it goes through arid places seeking rest and does not find it. Then it says, 'I will return to the house I left.' When it arrives, it finds the house unoccupied, swept clean and put in order. Then it goes and takes with it seven other spirits more wicked than itself, and they go in and live there. And the final condition of that person is worse than the first..." (Matthew 12:43-45 NIV).

When referring to cleaning and filling the house, both **internally and externally**, or—as previously mentioned—controlling one's environment, both **internally and externally**, we are referring to that which is within a person and that which is surrounding a person. For example, the internal environment of a person includes the mind, soul and spirit— from which we experience thought, perspective, emotions, attitude, character, values, love, etc., and the gateway to one's mind, soul, and spirit are the *eyes* and *ears*. Conversely, the external environment of a person, for instance, involves what is physically surrounding an individual like one's family, school, church, community, etc.— all of which have access to and influence on one's mind, soul, and spirit through the same eye and ear gateways. This is why it is vitally important to address **both** the *internal* and *external* factors of *cleaning and filling one's house* (or as previously mentioned, controlling one's internal and external environment)—and such efforts must be carried out intentionally (no luck involved), purposefully (not selfishly), strategically (no *"winging it"*), and aggressively (not passive or lackadaisically). In short, it will require a *"HYPERFOCUS"* on one's environment!

After pouring out all of the alcohol in my apartment, I then blocked all of the women who I was *"associating"* with, and then deleted each one of their numbers from my phone because I had never taken the time to remember their phone numbers. I cut off all toxic relationships and relationships with people who were doing things that I no longer wanted to do. Unfortunately, for myself, this included my own family— siblings and mother—because they were still drinking, drugging, and living with negative mentalities, so I did my best to love them, and honor them from a distance. I stopped listening to gangster rap and the sexually lustful R&B music that I would occasionally listen to in my "fallen" state. Instead, I would listen to Christian rap and Gospel music. I stopped watching television shows and movies that had half naked women, nudity, revenge and violence—and started watching more wholesome television shows and movies that were about family, love, kindness, and purpose (movies that would inspire me and also make me laugh).

> *"I cut off all toxic relationships and relationships with people who were doing things that I no longer wanted to do."*

The very next day—after pouring out the alcohol—on October 18, 2018 (a Thursday), I woke up and went to work. I had a list of properties to provide lawn care services for, and I had decided to do the work myself. I finished my route at approximately 1 PM and started my drive back towards my apartment. Outside of my control, my drive involved the passing of multiple liquor stores in the urban area in which I had lived. Out of nowhere, a voice speaking as clear as day said, "who do you think you are fooling? You know you are not going to be able to do this; you might as well just stop at a liquor store and grab a drink." As I continued my drive home, the voice only got louder and clearer—bombarding my mind with doubt and temptation. This voice began to remind me of all of the other times that I had tried to quit drinking but failed. Refusing to accept both the lies and truth that this voice was presenting, I drove to the church that I had previously attended and parked my truck in the parking lot. I then texted the Bishop of the church—who I had both a personal and business relationship with—and waited anxiously for his response. After approximately 20 minutes of waiting, while being bombarded by this voice of temptation, I started my truck and began to drive. Since the Bishop was unavailable, I reached out to my best friend—Clinton Lee Adams Jr. who is a Christian and Pastor. I explained to him that I had poured out all of the alcohol in my apartment the day before, and had taken a stand to regain my life and sobriety, but was overwhelmed by this voice and temptation to drink. Clint's first response was, "let me pray for you." As soon as Clint began to pray, the reception of the cell phone began to go in and out; I could no longer hear him speak/pray; the cellular connection was choppy. As soon as he finished praying, the cellular connection was restored, and his voice was clear again. I said, "bro, I could not hear anything that you were saying in that prayer because your reception was going in and out." Clint responded by informing me that the area that he was driving in had poor reception.

> *"After ending the phone call with Clint, while still driving down Blue Hill Avenue in Boston, God's voice spoke louder than the enemy's voice— saying, 'go to a church where there are cars in the parking lot.'"*

He said he would call me back later, when he was in a better area. Instantly, I knew this was the devil. The Bible states, "Again, truly I tell you that if two of you on earth agree about anything they ask for, it will be done for them by my Father in heaven" (Matthew 18:19 NIV). How could I agree with Clint's prayer, if I could not hear what he was saying? The Bible also refers to *satan* as being *"the prince of the power of the air"* (Ephesians 2:2 NKJV). This is why he was able to interfere with our cellular connection while Clint was praying. I do not want to digress too much, but I do want to point out that there are levels regarding prayer and levels regarding the power of prayer. Prayer is extremely powerful by itself; however, when combined with other biblical principles, the power of prayer is multiplied tremendously. For example, prayer combined with agreement (when two or more agree with you in prayer), prayer combined with fasting, prayer combined with praise, prayer combined with worship, are simply a few examples of how the power of prayer can be multiplied drastically.

After ending the phone call with Clint, while still driving down Blue Hill Avenue in Boston, God's voice spoke louder than the enemy's voice—saying, "go to a church where there are cars in the parking lot." Not only is it easy to find a liquor store in the hood (urban neighborhood), it is also very easy to find a church, if one is looking. However, finding one on a Thursday at approximately 4 PM with a parking lot filled with cars is different from finding one on a Sunday morning or afternoon. After passing a few churches with no cars in the parking lots— coming to the end of Blue Hill Avenue in Boston, right before it enters Milton Massachusetts— I looked to my left and saw *Jubilee Christian Church* with a parking lot filled with cars. I turned into the parking lot and parked my truck. Then I approached the main entrance of the church. Opening one of the front doors, I walked into an empty foyer. With doors to my left and right—and doors directly in front of me—I attempted to open each door, but every one of them was locked. While standing in an empty foyer, the Spirit of God moved upon me to go outside and check every perimeter door of the church. So I stepped outside of the main entrance and started walking around the church— trying to open every exterior door that I approached, but they all were locked. Finally, I approached a door that was towards the rear of the building, and when I pulled on the door it sprang open.

"I immediately felt the presence of God, and—this time—the doorway into the sanctuary was wide open."

I would later find out that a security guard who left for lunch— thinking that he had locked the door—had mistakenly left it open. The doorway led down to the basement, where I encountered a woman who was doing arts and crafts. I asked her if there was a Pastor in the building—telling her that I really needed to speak to a Pastor. Using her cell phone, she contacted security, who eventually brought me to a Pastor —Pastor Michael Manigault— an associate pastor at Jubilee Christian

Church in Boston. Pastor Mike and I spoke for approximately two hours. At the end of our conversation, he prayed for me and invited me to *"Morning Prayer"* the following day, at 6 AM. He had informed me that the church was open every morning at 6 AM for *Morning Prayer*—Monday through Saturday—and that the church held Sunday service at 7:30am, 10am, and 12:30pm. My first thought was that there was no way that I was going to leave my apartment early in the morning and drive to church just to pray at 6 AM. Before going our separate ways, Pastor Mike said, "give me three days." When I left the church, I did not understand what he meant. Was he asking me to give him three days without having a drink, was he asking me to come to *Morning Prayer* for three days straight? I was uncertain. The one thing I did know was that being in the house of God and praying with a man of God (ENVIRONMENT) silenced the voice that was tormenting me that day. The next morning, October 19, 2018 (a Friday), I decided to go to *Morning Prayer*. I entered that same empty foyer and could hear a woman singing worship music. I immediately felt the presence of God, and—this time—the doorway into the sanctuary was wide open. I walked into the sanctuary and went straight up to the altar— where I laid belly down on my face before God—and cried out for change. When *Morning Prayer* was over, *Pastor Mike* introduced me to the head Pastor of the church—Pastor Matthew K. Thompson— who would later become my Pastor and friend. The following morning, October 20, 2018 (a Saturday), I attended morning prayer again. On Sunday, October 21, 2018, I attended Sunday service, and to my surprise, the Pastor preached about me in front of thousands of people and pointed me out in the crowd. He preached about me trying to open every exterior door on the church and about Pastor Mike speaking with me for approximately two hours. He spoke about seeing me at *Morning Prayer* that Friday (October 19th) laying on my belly, face down, crying out to God. Then he prophetically declared in front of everyone that addiction had fallen off of my life.

A clip of this service can be seen on YouTube at:

https://youtu.be/bs_T1YKPlxo?si=Ejpa3HwYG6d3zMQa

On Monday morning, October 22, 2018–after morning prayer—I realized that it was day three of *Morning Prayer,* and I still had not had a drink. It had also dawned on me that I had not experienced a single withdrawal symptom from the alcohol or a temptation to drink. I knew, without a shadow of a doubt that God had delivered me from alcoholism completely, and "He who the Son sets free, is free indeed" (John 8:36). The following Sunday I was baptized— completely accepting and openly acknowledging this new life of sobriety. During the baptism ceremony, the head pastor, again, spoke a prophetic word over my life. This service can also be seen on YouTube at:

https://youtu.be/CVfcloWliHo?si=tWzXrVgAC7AN0YBr

I had attended Morning Prayer for 122 days straight before I missed my first *Morning Prayer* meeting since that very first day of me attending *Morning Prayer* on October 19, 2018 (ENVIRONMENT).

"Otherwise, 'the final condition of that person [will be] worse than the first...'" (Matthew 12:45 NIV).

Cleaning out the house and ridding it of all negativities is not enough; it MUST be filled with valuable items and people—so much so —that there isn't enough space for anything else. Otherwise, *"the final condition of that person [will be] worse than the first..."* (Matthew 12:45 NIV). As a landscaping professional, one of the things that I learned over the years regarding lawn care is how to have a beautiful lawn without weeds. You see, the best way to keep weeds out of your grass is to have a full, rich, and healthy lawn. In other words, simply ripping the weeds out of the lawn is not enough. For example, if there are dead spots (bald spots) in your lawn, the proper approach is to have rich soil in those areas to plant new grass seed. Once the grass seed begins to grow, the blades of grass are typically thin—until fertilized. Once fertilized, the blades of grass become fuller—leaving no room for weeds to grow. In fact, one of my favorite products for creating plush lawns is the yellow bag of Scotts fertilizer, "*Weed and Feed.*" I remember when I was a rookie landscaper, I thought to myself, "how can a product fertilize grass and kill weeds simultaneously?" I later learned that the killing of the weeds was not due to any poison, but to the richness and fullness of the lawn, which did not allow room/space for the weeds to grow and/or exist.

"But seek ye first the kingdom of God, and his righteousness; and all these things shall be added unto you" (Matthew 6:33 KJV).

As I continued to *fill my house* with church, positive people, Bible reading, books, prayer, and fasting (a hyperfocus on *the kingdom of God, and his righteousness)*— not only did God provide for my every need (physically, mentally, emotionally, psychologically, and spiritually), but He also started opening up doors of opportunity for me to step into *abundant living.*

"The thief does not come except to steal, and to kill, and to destroy. I have come that they may have life, and that they may have it more abundantly" (John 10:10 NKJV).

"Instead, I believe that my father was letting me know that I was his favorite—as Joseph was to his father Israel—and that despite having to suffer much, I too will do great things according to God's purpose and timing."

This is the transition that I was referring to at the beginning of this book—the transition from being the *survivor* that my mother spoke about to being triumphant and victorious—a *son with the colorful robe*—as my father had referred to me as. Anyone who knows the story of *Joseph*—"*the son with the colorful robe*"—knows that *Joseph* eventually governed all of Egypt's wealth and was the agent that God used to save his entire family (Genesis 37:3). No, I am not suggesting that I will be president or some type of world leader—nor was my father making such a claim. Instead, I believe that my father was letting me know that I was his favorite—as *Joseph* was to his father *Israel*—and that despite having to suffer much, I too will do great things according to God's purpose and timing. In regard to the above-mentioned transition, please do not be fooled into thinking that going from surviving to thriving is a one-time thing. In fact, many great men and woman will admit to experiencing such a transition several times throughout their lives—and in more than one area in their lives. For example, a marriage may transition from simply surviving to thriving—or a business may transition from simply surviving to thriving. In addition, someone's health and well-being may transition from surviving to thriving, and this can happen physically, mentally, emotionally, psychologically, and even spiritually—and more than once in one's life.

Another door that God opened—while "*seeking first the Kingdom of God and His Righteousness*" (and during the *cleaning & filling* process) —was a mentor/mentee relationship in my field of business (landscaping). My first business mentor was a man by the name of Lee Gilliam, owner of *Gilliam & Sons Landscaping* in *Waltham Massachusetts*. Lee had owned and operated his company for 30+ years and had a wealth of knowledge in the field. Knowing Lee, and having access to his knowledge and experience, expedited the growth of my landscaping company exponentially (environment). Furthermore, as a small business owner, I started to fill my house with other business owners and entrepreneurs. In addition, the intermingling and rubbing elbows with other business owners created an interest and curiosity regarding investing and other streams of income.

> *"The results of me placing a hyperfocus on my environment, produced a fruitful harvest."*

A Fruitful Harvest

The results of me placing a hyperfocus on my environment, produced a fruitful harvest. The landscaping company that I started in 2012– the one that I had almost driven into the ground while drinking and living recklessly— started to produce abundantly. The 122 days of *Morning Prayer* resulted in me meeting my wife, Suze— who also played a major role in my environment. She *"thought"* bigger than myself and exposed me to that thinking. For example, as a kid from the hood— who spent the majority of my life in the streets, homeless, in foster care, in juvenile correctional facilities, jail, and prison— the most I could have imagined was a small wedding with family and friends in a church. However, Suze thought much bigger than that. We had a big beautiful wedding that the two of us paid for without going into debt—due to Suze's thinking and strategizing. Being a kid from the hood, I had never left the country in my entire life. Suze—being a teacher for 15+ years with multiple degrees (a Bachelor's degree and two Masters)— had left the *United States* several times to visit other countries. My idea of a honeymoon would have been more along the lines of a weekend in *Vegas*, but Suze thought bigger than that. She insisted that we leave the country for a week, and I, on the other hand, had never owned a passport, nor did I even know where to obtain one. Having a woman like this in my environment resulted in me obtaining a passport and leaving the country for the first time in my life—at the age of 39 years old. I remember being nervous— due to my previous life of crime— wondering if I would get arrested at the border or prevented from leaving the country. As ridiculous as it may sound, it was my reality. Nonetheless, Suze and I enjoyed an amazing honeymoon in the Bahamas. Furthermore, when a small business investment went bad, and I had the opportunity to sell just to break even, Suze encouraged me to leverage the assets and start a second company which turned a small investment into six figures annually for two consecutive years— before I sold that second company (all while managing and growing my first company). And, last but not least, one of the greatest miracles and results of my hyperfocus on environment is our beautiful baby girl *Zanne*— born to Suze and I on Juneteenth 2020. If this is not a fruitful harvest, I don't know what is.

"Once I had created an all-around solid environment, my goal was to maintain, adjust, and upgrade that environment as necessary."

Maintain, Adjust, and Upgrade To Increase The Harvest

Once I had created an all-around solid environment, my goal was to *maintain, adjust,* and *upgrade* that environment as necessary. The importance of *maintaining, adjusting,* and *upgrading* one's environment cannot be emphasized enough— which is why it is one of the most important factors in *"the blueprint"* that I provide in the next chapter. In other words, my hyperfocus on business/finances, as I knew it, only got me so far. For example, it brought my landscaping company from four vehicles to ten vehicles— and from approximately 35 contracts to approximately 85 contracts. And it brought my car rental company, for instance, from three vehicles to approximately seven vehicles. A lot of this was accomplished with a *grind mentality* and an emphasis on work ethic (while being mentored by *TD Jakes* and *Eric Thomas* via YouTube, Pandora, and books) by prioritizing time and self-discipline —along with living honorably in business: character and integrity, so God could bless what I was doing.

"Your level of exposure will determine your level of success" (Environment).
~Jemal King ~

While *maintaining* a solid environment, one's hope is to never become stagnant—thus, the need to *adjust* and *upgrade*. In regards to business/finance, I went from reading books like *"So You Call Yourself A Man?"* and *"He-Motions"*—by *TD Jakes*—to *"Sore"* and *"Disruptive Thinking,"*(A New York Times Best Seller) by *TD Jakes* (*adjustment & upgrade*) —and from the *"Secret To Success"* by *Eric Thomas* to *"You Owe You"* (*A New York Times Best Seller*) by *Eric Thomas* (adjustment & upgrade). They placed an emphasis on expanding one's network and *getting the right information*—and God's desire for His children to *live in abundance* and experience financial freedom versus living in lack and in debt. I later learned about the *"Secret To Success"* podcast hosted by *CJ Quinney* and *Karl Wesley Phillips*— the creators of the *Eric Thomas* brand— who introduced *Jemal King* (*"The 9 to 5 Millionaire"*) to the world. One of *Jemal King's* famous sayings is *"Your level of exposure will determine your level of success"* (environment). They call him *The 9 to 5 Millionaire* because he kept his 9 to 5 job as a *Chicago* police officer for 20 years while investing in real estate. Real estate was something that I was always interested in since my early 20's because my uncle, Greg Gaffney, was a real estate investor and millionaire before losing everything to an ugly divorce and the drug overdose of his daughter/only child. When *Jemal King* launched his course and program called *"Make Real Estate Real"*, I bought the course for $1,000 and enrolled in the program— investing in oneself (which is also in *the blueprint* that I provide in the next chapter) is extremely important. *Jemal King* created this course and program using experts and members of his own real *estate team* including real estate attorneys (Damon Stewart and Adrian Zeno), lenders and loan officers (Mark Buffered and Natasha Robinson), brokerage owners and operators (Perdure "Koach" Carter and April C. Troope), credit expert (Terri Couser), life insurance expert/agent (Nathan Majors), and so many more. The *"Make Real Estate Real"* course/program did not only place a hyperfocus on financial freedom, but also on *generational wealth*. They taught about real estate investing, trust funds, life insurance, personal and business credit, retirement, etc..— with a hyperfocus on *getting the right information*. Furthermore, I read books like *"Rich Dad Poor Dad"* and *"Fake"*—books written by Robert T. Kiyosaki *(Also A New York Times Best Seller Author)* —and *"Take The Stairs"* *(A New York Times Best Seller)* by Rory Vaden. Towards the end of this book, I will also provide a list of suggested books to read (*My Top 20 Books*).

All in all, the repetitive cycle of *maintaining, adjusting,* and *upgrading* to increase the harvest was extremely fruitful. The landscaping company went from 10 to 19 vehicles (12 owned and 7 financed) in a couple of years and from approximately 85 contracts to approximately 200 contracts. The car rental company went from approximately seven vehicles to 18 vehicles (all owned—not leased or financed) in the first year of business. With businesses containing 30+ vehicles, it only made sense for me to start an additional company—a tow truck company. This company, however, due to some unforeseen circumstances, had to be shut down. Nonetheless, my attention toward *maintaining, adjusting,* and *upgrading* led me to starting a fourth business (in the same year) as a real estate investor— resulting in me purchasing my first investment property: a six-unit commercial building in *Chicago, Illinois (thanks to God, Eric Thomas, Jemal King, Perdure Carter, Terri Couser, Attorney Adrian Zeno, Attorney Antonia Mills, and more).*

> *"As the harvest increased, my family and I got to do things and experience things that I could have never imagined."*

As the harvest increased, my family and I got to do things and experience things that I could have never imagined. We were able to travel often and experience some (not all) of the finer things in life. For example, on our anniversary, I was able to take my wife to the *Château at Nemacolin* in Pennsylvania— where we stayed in the presidential suite (where US Presidents and celebrities stayed) which came with a butler for $3k+ a night. I had my wife pampered from head to toe— facial, massage, and body wrap before an amazing dining experience.

While we were there, in Pennsylvania, I blew her mind by taking her to *Falling Waters* where we walked through some of the homes built by the famous architect: Frank Lloyd Wright. My wife is somewhat of an intellectual who loves history and art. To some, life like this is normal or *"no big deal,"* but for me—a kid from the hood who grew up in poverty living off welfare, food stamps, and section 8- this type of living was beyond what I could imagine. I went from barely ever traveling to traveling often—*FIRST CLASS*. I was able to upgrade my wife's wedding ring, pay off approximately $60k in school loans in a single transaction—CASH (not credit), provide minor upgrades to our home and property, purchase my first life insurance policy worth 1.4 million, and (of course) buy myself a couple of little toys— another motorcycle and *slingshot*.

Most importantly, this increase in harvest meant that I could not only be a blessing to my family and friends, but I could also be a blessing to others. It allowed me to give more jobs to people in need and be a financial blessing to churches and other Christians. When one of my best friends/brothers—*Thomas E. Koonce*—was released from prison after serving 30 years, I was able to pay his rent for a year until he was able to get on his feet. Today, he is extremely successful, and I am convinced that the world will hear his story as well. In addition, the harvest increase allowed me to start a fifth business to created impact and encourage change. I threw my first conference in the hood at the *Salvation Army Ray and Joan Kroc Corps Community Center* in Boston— the very place where I got my first job (at $11.00 an hour) once released from prison. To come full circle (10 years later)—being there throwing a conference on personal and business development—was a humbling experience. Not to mention being there after going from $11 an hour to over a million in revenue—TO GOD BE ALL THE GLORY. Please check out the YouTube links that highlight the conference.

https://youtu.be/c-Lyn5KPGuA?si=YhjW8fKznaRE6X6f

https://youtu.be/C5EmJZ2yHlc?si=iogisz3LMrs8GxwT

https://youtu.be/fzVOrZ7bTEo?si=DaDdu4Q3j9x20Op0

Who's The Master? I Am!

The words, "Who's the master? I am!" are words from a 1985 movie titled *The Last Dragon*. At this point in my life, I am a *Master Farmer/ Gardener*—an expert in the field of environment. After watching and experiencing the results of a hyperfocus on environment—while incarcerated— then, watching and experiencing the results of a hyperfocus on environment —once released back into society—then watching and experiencing the results of a hyperfocus on environment after experiencing life altering circumstances (like my son's adoption, Crystal's affair and the divorce, an alcohol addiction that almost killed me several times, a serious bout with depression and suicidal thoughts, drugs, and the death of both my father and grandmother in the same month)—I am convinced that anyone can revolutionize their life by understanding the *absolute severity of environment* and placing a hyperfocus on their internal and external environments. In other words, it worked in prison; it worked in society, and it worked when I was in one of the darkest places of my life—so it will absolutely work for you if applied (no matter the situation or circumstance).

> *"Today, as an expert on environment—a Master Farmer/Gardener— I understand the absolute severity of environment."*

Today, as an expert on environment—a *Master Farmer/Gardener*— I understand *the absolute severity of environment*. It is said that an expert is someone who has spent approximately 10,000 hours studying and practicing a specific skill or subject. Some even say that the number of hours spent studying and practicing is double that—ranging between 20,000 hours and 25,000 hours. Before getting discouraged by these numbers, please note that these numbers are extremely low in comparison to the person who makes the focus of environment a part of their *everyday* life. I started my focus on environment (internally and externally) in the beginning of 2003, when I was 22 years old; today, I am 43 years old as I write the words in this book. With well over 100,000 hours of education and experience (study & practice) in the field of environment—in the last 21 years of my life— I am happy to share my *blueprint* for becoming a *Master Farmer/Gardener*. Furthermore, I believe that if you are living, you are learning. Therefore, I will go as far as to say that during the first 22 years of my life, I was also learning and experiencing (consciously and unconsciously) the effects of environment (MORE HOURS). Moreover, if you are at least 20 years of age while reading this book, I am willing to credit you 5000 hours of learning and experience (study & practice) at the *University of Environment*. This means that you are almost halfway there—to becoming a *Master Farmer/Gardener*. More specifically, after 20 years of living— and reading the first eight chapters of this book— there is no way that you are not able to identify how your environments have shaped your life, who you are, and where you are at regarding multiple aspects of life. If you are at least 15 years of age—while reading this book— you too will get a credit (of 2500 hours) at the *University of Environment*.

CHAPTER 9

CREATING YOUR ENVIRONMENT

*"Surely you need guidance to wage war,
and victory is won through many advisers."*
(Proverbs 24:6)

What Seed – What Soil?

"That same day Jesus went out of the house and sat by the lake. Such large crowds gathered around him that he got into a boat and sat in it, while all the people stood on the shore. Then he told them many things in parables, saying: 'A farmer went out to sow his seed. As he was scattering the seed, some fell along the path, and the birds came and ate it up. Some fell on rocky places, where it did not have much soil. It sprang up quickly, because the soil was shallow. But when the sun came up, the plants were scorched, and they withered because they had no root. Other seed fell among thorns, which grew up and choked the plants. Still other seed fell on good soil, where it produced a crop—a hundred, sixty or thirty times what was sown. Whoever has ears, let them hear'"
(Matthew 13:1-9 NIV).

In this specific Bible scripture, Jesus is pointing out the *absolute severity of environment.* There is no mention of the seed being *"good seed"* or *"bad seed"*— instead, the main and *only* focus is the condition of the environment which will determine the growth and development of the seed.

"Listen then to what the parable of the sower means: When anyone hears the message about the kingdom and does not understand it, the evil one comes and snatches away what was sown in their heart. This is the seed sown along the path. The seed falling on rocky ground refers to someone who hears the word and at once receives it with joy. But since they have no root, they last only a short time. When trouble or persecution comes because of the word, they quickly fall away. The seed falling among the thorns refers to someone who hears the word, but the worries of this life and the deceitfulness of wealth choke the word, making it unfruitful. But the seed falling on good soil refers to someone who hears the word and understands it. This is the one who produces a crop, yielding a hundred, sixty or thirty times what was sown"
(Matthew 13:18-23 NIV).

The Blueprint

1.) Understanding It's Possible and Having a Why:
In my opinion, *understanding it's possible* is the chicken, and *having a why* is the egg (the chicken or the egg?).   I have heard some of the *greats* explain the importance of having a *why*. Although, I do agree with the fact that *having a why* is essential, for me, *understanding it's possible* was just as important/crucial. For example, my *why* was easy to identify—I knew that God wanted better for myself, and I knew that my children were dependent upon me being better and doing better—however, I had to come to the realization that doing *better* was actually a possibility for someone like myself. In other words, there are lots of people in the world who want *better*, but because they do not believe that better is possible, they do not even make an effort towards obtaining "*it*" (better)— whatever "*it*" may be. Instead, they become complacent and accept things as they are. They become hopeless; thinking— "this is the way things are, so this is the way things are going to remain." They accept the hand they were dealt. They may even complain about their current situation— finding fault and placing blame on the "*white man,*" the "*system,*" their parents, or someone else who may have hurt or harmed them— but they take no action to create change because they simply do not believe that change is possible.

More specifically, in the environment that I grew up in, for instance, it was common for men (pimps, drug dealers, and even the "average Joe's") to have multiple children by multiple women without acknowledging and/or living up to their responsibility to take care of those children. In my opinion, these men had their *why*, but their *why* was not enough. Why? Because they had accepted their reality—situations and circumstances—as being something that was impossible for them to change. When I heard *Eric Thomas* lecture on the importance of having a *why*, it resonated with me deeply. Likewise, when I heard him speak about being born to a teenage mother, hating school, not being a good reader or writer, ending up homeless, and it taking him twelve years to obtain a four-year degree— it resonated with me just as much. He spoke about not having to be the smartest or most talented individual in the room, but being willing to be the hardest working individual in the room. He emphasized being the first one to show up and the last one to leave—about not having to be magna cum laude or summa cum laude, but simply getting to the *spot* before they get to the *spot*— and today he has a *PhD* and is considered the number one motivational speaker in the world. It was this *understanding of it being possible* that was the fuel (for me) that—when combined with the spark of my *why*—ignited my pursuit of being the best version of myself that I could possibly be.

2.) Start Where You're At—START TODAY:

I started as a 22-year-old young man in county jail. Yes, in a controlled environment, I chose to control my environment by starting the *cleaning & filling* process of my *internal and external* environments (Hyperfocus).

3.) Understand, Test, and Manipulate:

Master Farmers/Gardeners know that soil is made up of minerals, organic minerals, water, and air. Moreover, the appropriate balance of nutrients and texture is crucial regarding the richness of the soil. Therefore, both farmers and gardeners go to great lengths to **understand**, **test**, and **manipulate** their soil for optimal results. Therefore, it is essential that we *understand*, *test*, and *manipulate* the elements of our environments, as well.

Understanding may involve a deeper look at oneself, personality, values, habits, likes, and dislikes—along with one's family, upbringing, culture, community, and experiences.

Testing will require evaluation— what people, places, and/or things are bringing you down, instead of bringing you up? For the Christian, it will be what people, places, and/or things are bringing you closer to God and His purpose for your life?

Manipulating is the process of *cleaning and filling*— removing the people, places, and/or things that are unhealthy and unproductive, and adding new people, places, and/or things that are healthy and productive.

4.) Identifying Master Farmer/Gardeners and Where They Can Be Found:

This is actually easy for some: school and college (High-School Diploma, Bachelor's Degree, Master's Degree, PhD). In these environments, you will find coaches, teachers, college professors, and a network of intellectuals in a variety of different fields. However, not only is it true that *college is not for everyone*, but college may be too expensive for some—*at the moment*. I say, "*at the moment*" because I have heard too many stories about people getting their degrees later on in life—in their 40s, 50s, and 60s even. In fact, I did not start college until the age of 27, and I did so with a GED (not a high school diploma). Yes, there is financial aid and student loans, but sometimes financial aid is only that—an aid that includes a balance that must be paid— and student loans must be paid back with interest. Don't get me wrong, if college is for you, and somehow you can afford it—GO FOR IT!

Nonetheless, there is a large population who believes that college is not for them, and it is important for them to know that greatness is. More importantly, that greatness can and must be obtained through environment by having access to *Master Farmer/Gardeners*.

A.) First, you have to be looking for them (*Master Farmer/Gardeners*).

B.) Second, you have to know what to look for.

Let's start by viewing the definition of *master:*

Adjective: *"having or showing very great skill or proficiency."*

Verb: *"acquire complete knowledge or skill in an accomplishment, technique, or art."*

I would like to point out the words, *great skill* and *proficiency* along with *complete knowledge.*

Simply put, find the *best of the best* where you are at, and, specifically, in the areas in which you would like to grow. If I could do this in prison, you can do this anywhere. To put it bluntly, if you are the smartest person in your circle—**GET OUT OF THAT CIRCLE!**

Today, *Master Farmer/Gardeners* are easier to find than ever before —with the World Wide Web, social media, etc... I do recommend that you do your research because there are lots of wannabe (want-to-be) *Master Farmer/Gardeners* out there who only want to swindle you for money or some other hidden agenda.

5.) Making Master Farmer/Gardeners a Part of YOUR Environment:
Somehow bring them into your environment, so you can learn and practice their habits, instructions, and strategies as much as possible.

FREE:
A friend of mine who was starting his own construction company told me a story about how he learned how to build stone patios. He told me how he hid in the bushes while watching another man build a patio. Eventually, the man saw him and yelled, "Hey, what are you doing over there?" and he (my friend) said, "I'm sorry man; I just wanted to learn how to build a patio," and the gentleman said, "well, why didn't you just ask"—and then invited him over to watch up close

and personal while he provided a detailed narrative/tutorial on how to build a patio.

The moral of the story is, you will be surprised to know how many people would love to share their knowledge and passion regarding their expertise.

When I started my first company as a landscaper, *Lee Gilliam* was a major asset in my development and growth as a business owner. Although I owned my own landscaping company, I would still go work for his company to learn from him and his crew members. I would call him regularly to ask him questions about business—"how should I do this" and "how should I do that?" At first, I was concerned that I may be bothering him. I later learned that Lee had sons, and he wished that his sons would call him as often as I did with an interest and passion for landscaping as well.

We are all too aware of the *haters* in life—those who do not want to see us succeed or help us get there. However, when I placed a *hyperfocus* on my environment, I was shocked to realize how many people—*Master Farmer/Gardeners*—who were willing to share their wealth of knowledge.

One of the *Master Farmer/Gardeners* who is in my life is my godmother the *Honorable Christina Harms*—a retired probate court judge for 23 years. Furthermore, I cannot take any credit for her being in my life because (I believe God ordained our relationship) there were too many unknown factors that were outside of my control. You see, after passing the exam and getting accepted into Boston University (while incarcerated), I then applied for a program called *Partakers*. *Partakers* was limited and only accepting certain applicants, so the requirements included a written essay explaining the desire for a team of educational mentors. Writing the essay did not guarantee that I would be chosen; then, once chosen, someone had to assign a team of mentors to me out of a larger pool of *Master Farmer/Gardeners*. In short, there were too many elements left to chance— that's why I truly believe that God ordained our relationship. Her role—and the role of the *Partakers* team that was assigned to me—was to simply assist with my studies at *Boston University*, and as you can see throughout this book— for whatever reasons—they went above and beyond the call of duty.

More importantly, I do not recommend that anyone sit around and wait for a chance in regard to making *Master Farmer/Gardeners* a part of their environment.

More specifically, I listened to *Eric Thomas* for approximately three years (for free) on Pandora and YouTube— learning and practicing his habits, instructions, and strategies—before I could afford to attend his functions. The things that I was learning and practicing, helped me further grow and develop as a person, husband, father, and entrepreneur.

The same could be said about *TD Jakes* regarding the first conference I attended in 2012–the *Man Power* conference—when a Christian brother by the name of Larry Wyche walked around with an envelope at his church, *Holy Tabernacle Church* in Boston, asking brothers to chip in so that I could attend the *2012 Man Power* conference in *Dallas Texas*. In addition, I watched *TD Jakes* sermons in prison for years, and read several of his books—books that I had borrowed from other men who I was incarcerated with.

The point I am trying to make is that you can make some of the best *Master Farmer/Gardeners* in the world a part of your environment, and you can do it for free without ever having to meet them in person or attend one of their events—no cost at all means NO EXCUSES!

You can gain access to some for free via relationships—coaches, teachers, pastors, mentors, *Big Brother and Big Sister Agencies*, as well as material posted on Pandora, YouTube, and other social media platforms —along with borrowed books and the World Wide Web.

Invest In Yourself:

I believe God's purpose is for people to be whole—healed and complete—physically, mentally, emotionally, psychologically, spiritually, and even financially. So, while your chosen *Master Farmer/Gardeners* are helping you grow and develop as a person, husband, wife, father, mother, leader, entrepreneur, etc., you can expect your finances to grow simultaneously— placing you in a position to be able to invest in yourself via college, trade training, courses, seminars, books, paid coaching, and mentorships, etc.. In the previous chapter, I shared how I spent $1,000 on *Jemal King's "Make Real Estate Real"* course/program. Completing the course made me an "alumni," so when *Jemal King* and *ETA* (*Eric Thomas & Associates*) threw their first weeklong *Make Real Estate Real "family reunion"* in Mexico, I was eligible to attend. I invested approximately $10k between the VIP tickets that I purchased, flight, and stay. I "*got in the room*" with the experts, obtained much more information, networked with others, and was motivated and inspired by so many other likeminded individuals. Simply put, I invested in myself. It was during that event that I met *Eric Thomas* for the first time, in person. In the previous chapter, I shared some details about the time in which my wife and I went to Pennsylvania for our anniversary. It was during that drive that my wife and I were conversing about going to the *"Make Real Estate Real Family Reunion"* in Mexico, and I told her that I knew that Eric Thomas, CJ, and Karl we're also going to be there— and that, somehow, I was going to leave with a relationship with them. She looked at me like I was crazy, and I said, "I am not going to be satisfied with simply attending the conference and taking pictures with *Jemal King* and the *ETA* family just so I can post it on Facebook and say that I attended—no, when I leave, I am going to leave with a relationship with *Jemal King* and the *ETA* family." This was in August— two months before the weeklong *family reunion*/conference and two months before ever meeting *Jemal King, Eric Thomas, CJ*

Quinney, and *Karl Wesley Phillips*. Now we can fast forward to the first day in Mexico. After everyone arrived and got settled, there was a special *"meet and greet"* scheduled with music and refreshments. While everyone was mingling and taking in the experience, my wife and I found a spot to relax. It wasn't long before *Jemal, CJ*, and *Karl* entered the room. As one can imagine, everyone flocked around them to introduce themselves, take pictures, and socialize. I just began to pray. Suddenly, my wife nudged me— as if she completely forgot about what I said to her two months prior to the event—*"Nickolas"* she said, *"Look, it's Karl. Go take a picture with him."* My wife knew how much I love and follow the ETA crew and *The Secret To Success* podcast. When I looked up, Karl was standing two feet in front of me, but I just continued to pray. Knowing how it was Jemal King's event— and seeing how people were competing to have a moment of his time— I just stood back and continued to pray. When Jemal finished speaking with one person— before a full second could pass— someone else jumped in to speak with him immediately. Still having absolutely no idea how I was going to stand out in the bunch (among 200+ other people)—and initiate a conversation that would allow me to leave with a personal relationship— I just stood there and continued to pray.

Quick digression: before the event, I was so determined to make sure that I stood out amongst the crowd that I had a T-shirt made for every day of the week— T-shirts that had slogans/inside jokes that only *Jemal King, Eric Thomas, CJ, Karl*, and *"Secret To Success"* podcast followers would understand. I had five T-shirts made because two of the seven days were special events that required a specific dress code— an *all-white event* that required white clothing and the final evening dinner that required black and gold attire. The T-shirts read, "Doobie Actions-Doobie Consequences," "A5 Effort-A5 Results," "Left Side Living By The Grace of God," "Yellow Cake With Chocolate Frosting Is Chocolate Cake If You Are At Harold's Chicken," and last but not least *"You Owe You."*

As people circled around *Jemal*, the same scenario just continued to repeat itself— as soon as he wrapped up a conversation with one person—before a full second could pass—someone else would jump in with lightning speed. I just continued to *"watch and pray"* (Matthew 26:41a). Finally, God spoke to me, *"son just be yourself and do what Nick would do."* Right then, I walked through the crowd and tapped Jemal on his shoulder and said, *"Hey Mal, when you're done talking, can I have a minute"*? His response was, *"absolutely."* When he finished speaking to the individual that he was conversing with— before a full second could pass—another individual jumped in to converse with him. But this time, he stopped the individual and said, *"give me a minute,"* and then he turned around directly to me and said, *"Hey man, what's up?"* Now, with the full attention of a multi-millionaire, I introduced myself and shared with him that people do not believe me when I say that one of my role models is a police officer; then, I quickly shared a real estate obstacle that I was facing since completing his course. He looked me in the eyes and said, *"I got you; give me your phone."* I handed him my phone with no questions asked, and he dialed his cell phone number into my phone. Then he looked me in the eyes again and said, *"I got you; this is my real number, the only number I have."* I said, *"thanks brother; I really appreciate you."* I walked back over to my wife, and Jemal continued to mingle. At that point, I was satisfied for the evening. The first day of the event—and within the first hour of our *meet and greet*— I had obtained the personal cell phone number of a multi-millionaire. As a kid from the hood who grew up poor, this was a lot to digest. Silently, I went back into prayer—praising God, and thanking Him for all that He had done and was going to do in my life. With a smile on my face—and on my heart— I was ready to enjoy the rest of the evening, mingling and taking pictures. Taking the advice of my wife, I got a picture with Karl and a picture with CJ before the night came to an end. Why did I share these details with you, and what do I hope you will gain? Well, I'm glad you asked. However, the real question is *how far are you willing to go* (silly T-shirts) and *how much are you willing to invest in yourself—for yourself and for those who you love?* **We're not done yet!**

My next investment came as a surprise even to me. I'll explain. One might think that I should have been content with having the personal cell phone number of *Jemal King*. As excited and thankful as I was, my goal was to also have a relationship with ETA— which meant that, somehow, I was going to have to stand out from the bunch in the eyes of *Eric Thomas, CJ* or *Karl*. My T-shirts were gaining attention by some, but not enough to make a lasting impression. While we were enjoying this amazing resort at the *Xcaret* in Mexico, I would start every morning as usual in prayer. One morning, while asking God what I should do to ensure that I will leave the place with a relationship with *ETA*, God's response to me in prayer was, "use what's in your hand"— the very words He spoke to Moses in the Bible (Exodus 4:2-9). When He spoke those words, He showed me a vision of the little blue bank bag that I had filled with cash. I had brought this cash for my wife and I. Despite having credit cards and debit cards, I did not feel safe leaving the country without cash, and my intention was to splurge on my wife and I. Nonetheless, I planned to be obedient. Later on that day, God had provided an opportunity for me to speak to *Eric Thomas* in person regarding a personal matter. In that conversation, he too had given me his personal cell phone number. Remembering the blue bag, I said, *"wait here, I have a gift for you,"* and that day I gave him $10k as a gift. He was just as shocked as I was. He would later text me and tell me to meet him at the beach at 6 AM on Saturday—which I did—and that was the beginning of my relationship with *Eric Thomas*. You can see both of us talking about this day in the YouTube videos provided below.

https://youtu.be/3yGHf48_qH0?si=xRu-bIDQKhj_DTmb

https://youtu.be/Fa4KOk_aK78?si=DApFJMTdGHjrFNUI

https://youtu.be/2dneVbZj3f8?si=4aqidNZWKCvL04Fs

https://youtu.be/gqDZ3bv1OEQ?si=DKgJI20xyXVRMMdJ

He speaks about not being impressed with the $10k (being some-one who gets paid six figures to speak for less than an hour—and being someone who gets paid six figures for being the personal coach of professional athletes), but being more impressed about the gesture coming from a kid from the hood, with the background that I have, and being a person who had to work hard for his money (the sacrifice). More specifically, I personally believe that we are supposed to feed what feeds us. As a result, we create an endless cycle of reciprocity. Overall, I accomplished what I set out to do— by investing in myself I left Mexico with a personal relationship with *Jemal King*, *Eric Thomas*, and *ETA*. I followed them for three years for free on social media before ever attending an event and/or meeting them in person. As a result, I watch my life go from one level to the next. In short, I made them a part of my environment for free. Since investing in myself, meeting them in person, and having a relationship with them, they have assisted in my learning, growing, and developing in many different areas of life, they helped me purchase my first six unit commercial building in *Chicago Illinois*, they have supported me and encouraged me often, and as of recently *Eric Thomas* is writing the foreword for this book. To have the number one motivational speaker in the world writing the foreword to my book—priceless.

I did the same thing when I placed a hyperfocus on my credit, both personal and business. I followed the teachings of an expert—*Terri Couser* from "*Care Credit Tools*"—a credit guru who used to work for the credit bureaus. I followed her for approximately two years for free on social media; then, hired her as a personal credit coach. She helped me establish business credit and take my personal credit from a 500 to an 800. Moreover, I learned about Terri through *Jemal King's* course, and learned about Jemal through *Eric Thomas* and the *Secret To Success* podcast. What's my point? Glad you asked. When you get around gurus, you will meet other gurus. Or should I say, when you get around *Master Farmer/Gardeners*, you will meet other *Master Farmer/ Gardeners*.

Overall, the goal is to make *Master Farmer/Gardeners* a part of your environment, and the fact that it can be done for free leaves no excuse for anyone. Once you have maximized all of the possible growth for free—it might be time to adjust and upgrade to investing in self. This brings us to the next step of the *blueprint*—maintain, adjust, and upgrade.

6.) Maintain, Adjust, and Upgrade To Increase The Harvest:
Once you have created a solid environment that is producing a great harvest, the goal is to maintain it, adjust it, and upgrade it as necessary to increase the harvest. All of the details regarding this process can be found in chapter 8—pages 116 – 119.

7.) For Self & Future Generations:
As previously mentioned, both farmers and gardeners not only recognize and understand the importance of environment when planting seed and nurturing agriculture—their focus is on the positive outcome of the blossom: fruit, vegetables, flower, or rearing healthy animals. In fact, their (farmers and gardeners) model is, "soil is everything" (ENVIRONMENT). These *farmers* and *gardeners* are visionaries who strategically and diligently work the ground (soil) during a specific season in the hopes of reaping a harvest. They are the same visionaries mentioned previously who place their children in private schools and prepare them for college life. They do their best to create a positive and thriving environment for their children to grow up in. Furthermore, even if you are not a parent, you do have a moral responsibility as a *Master Farmer/Gardener* to pass what you have learned on to the next generation. More specifically, as previously mentioned—and known by

many—college is not for everyone, nor is it the only way to become a *Master Farmer/Gardener*. So, it is important that we create little master farmer/gardeners by assisting the development of their environments—even if college is not for them. Listed below are a few *"sub-environments"* (other than college) that can be used in creating healthy environments for oneself and the next generation:

Internal: Bible, Books, Music, Online Courses, Phone Therapy, Zoom Therapy, Videos, YouTube, and other Social Media content, etc.

External: Church, Sunday School, Bible Camp, Five-Fold Ministry, Big Brother/Big Sister, Mentorships, Paid Coaching, Conferences, Sports, Arts, Trade Training, Job Corps, ROTC, Military, Navy, Army, Counseling/Therapy, etc.

Be Intentional

Make no mistake; changing my environment did not happen overnight, and although, approximately 90% of the people who are currently in my environment were hand-picked, some of them (approximately 10%) came into my life by what some would call "happenstance." Now, I personally do not believe in happenstance; I believe that we all *reap what we sow* (Galatians 6:7-8), so although some may refer to this as karma— while on a journey to do good, the universe responded by bringing good people into my life— I; however, believe—due to my Christian roots—that God promises to put good people in our lives. But regardless of our belief systems, when you come across good people who add value to your life, you keep them. You add value to their lives in return, and you nurture those relationships because—in this world— they are hard to come by.

CHAPTER 10

FINAL THOUGHTS

”*Where there is strife, there is pride,*
but wisdom is found in those who take advice.“
(Proverbs 13:10)

Conclusion

In conclusion, it is important, essential, and even crucial that an individual understand the *absolute severity of environment*. Furthermore, a person who does not take their environment seriously is a person who does not value themself or the ones who are dependent upon them— loved ones and friends.

A nutritious environment is so important and necessary that there is not a single *"successful"* individual on the face of this planet who has obtained success without it. In fact, environment is so crucial that even God refused to do miracles in certain environments.

This book not only illustrates the damage created by a poor environment, it provides step-by-step examples and detailed instructions on how to create a powerful environment for oneself by becoming a *Master Farmer/Gardener* for self and future generations—and that, my friends, is how you master retention and recidivism prevention.

Your Invitation

Lastly, I wouldn't be me if I did not offer you the greatest invitation of all time—an invitation to the greatest *environment* that exists, *THE KINGDOM OF HEAVEN*. It would be as if you were walking down a completely dark alley—heading towards a hole with a mile long/deadly drop— and I knew about the dark alley and hole, but said nothing, remained silent, and allowed your death to take place. Not only would your blood be on my hands, I would be held accountable by my Heavenly Father.

So I present to you the greatest invitation that you will ever receive— with a very quick and simple prayer:

"Heavenly Father, I come to you now, in the name of Your Son *Jesus Christ of Nazareth*. I thank You for sending Your *Son Jesus Christ* to die on the cross for my sins and salvation because I could never earn a place in your Kingdom. According to Your Word and Promise— stated in Romans 10:9–I declare with my mouth that *Jesus is Lord*, and I believe in my heart that You *raised Him from the dead*, and I now receive Your gift of Salvation."

CONGRATULATIONS.

If you prayed that prayer, you have now guaranteed a place for yourself in the Kingdom of Heaven— the greatest *environment* to ever exist. And you have become a part of the greatest family to ever exist. We are not perfect here on earth, but we will be in heaven. Can't wait to see you there.

If you do not have a lot of experience reading the Bible, I suggest that you start at the beginning of the *New Testament* and read it two or three times before you start to read the *Old Testament*. Also, before you begin to read, I recommend that you say a quick prayer simply asking God to help you understand what you are about to read. The prayer can go as follows: "I come to You now, in the Name of *Jesus Christ of Nazareth*, asking you Father to help me understand what I am about to read—in *Jesus Name* I pray, Amen."

Reading 1 to 3 chapters daily is highly recommended. I also recommend that you read one chapter of *Psalms* and one chapter of *Proverbs*—daily, and you will literally start to see the Power of God, invade your life.

My Top 20 Books

The Absolute Severity of Environment *By Nickolas DeJarnette*	***Take The Stairs*** *By Rory Vaden*
So You Call Yourself A Man? *By T.D. Jakes*	***Balance*** *By Toure Roberts*
Battlefield of The Mind *By Joyce Meyers*	***He-Motions*** *By T.D. Jakes*
Rich Dad Poor Dad *By Robert T. Kiyosaki*	***The Purpose Driven Life*** *By Rick Warren*
You Owe You *By Eric Thomas*	***Disruptive Thinking*** *By T.D. Jakes*
Fake *By Robert T. Kiyosaki*	***9 to 5 Millionaire*** *By Jemal King*
Soar *By T.D. Jakes*	***Think You'll Be Happy*** *By Nicole Avant*
The Secret To Success *By Eric Thomas*	***Why? Because You're Anointed*** *By T.D. Jakes*
Crushing *By T.D. Jakes*	***Let It Go*** *By T.D. Jakes*
Healing The Wounds of The Past *By T.D. Jakes*	***INSTINCT*** *By T.D. Jakes*

A Quick Guide To Answered Prayer

I tell people often that the Bible is like a car manual. For example, a car manual will state that a specific car will give you so many miles per gallon. But if you turn the page, you will also read that the car needs a specific type of oil. If you turn the page again, you will find that the vehicle also needs transmission fluid. If you continue turning the pages you will read that the vehicle will also need antifreeze, so that the engine does not overheat. You will read that the tires must have a certain PSI (pounds per square inch) level of air pressure. Therefore, even if you completely fill the entire tank with gasoline, but have not done any *one* of the other things, the vehicle will not give you the expected miles per gallon. If you don't believe me, just ask any mechanic.

> "I tell people often that the Bible is like a car manual."

Let's use a Ford focus for example, which is expected to get 28 miles per gallon on city streets and 40 miles per gallon on highway roads—with a 12-gallon tank. If we do the math, we can see that the vehicle—with a filled tank—should get us 336 miles on city streets and 480 miles on highway roads. Now, ask a mechanic, if you fill up the Ford Focus with the best gasoline, will you still get the expected miles if there is no oil in the engine. The mechanic would not only inform you that you would not get the expected miles per gallon in a vehicle that never had oil in it, he would tell you what kind of damage you would cause to the engine. Then, ask that same mechanic, if you would still get the expected miles if the vehicle did not have any transmission fluid in the transmission. In this case, the vehicle would not move at all because the transmission fluid is what makes the gears engage for the vehicle to drive forward or backwards. If you are still not convinced, ask the mechanic what would happen if you tried to drive that vehicle the expected miles per gallon without any antifreeze in the radiator. Well, without being a mechanic, if you have ever owned a car, you already know that the engine would overheat. Lastly, I will address the air in the tires. Now it is obvious, if there was no air in the tires, the vehicle could still drive—damaging the rims—but doing so would cause the vehicle/engine to work harder, resulting in less miles per gallon because the vehicle would be burning more fuel than necessary. This is true, even if there was air in the tires. For instance, if there is *too much* air in the tires, the tires could pop, and if there is *not enough* air in the tires again, the vehicle/engine would have to overwork to compensate this inconsistency—resulting in the engine burning more gas and you getting less miles per gallon; consequently, not getting the expected amount of miles per gallon of gasoline.

In the same way, the Bible is similar to a car manual. There are many scriptures throughout the Bible that teach about prayer, for example. Mark 11:24 states, *"therefore, I say to you, whatever things you ask when you pray, believe that you receive them, and you will have them."* In this scripture, the requirement is *faith*—*"believing that you"* have already [received it] in order to receive it. Let's look at another example from another page. 1 John 5:14-15 states, *"Now this is the confidence that we have in Him, that if we ask anything according to His will, He hears us. And if we know that He hears us, whatever we ask, we know that we have the petitions that we have asked of Him."* Here we can see that *answered prayer* is dependent upon us asking for *"anything"* that is *"according to His will."*

> "There are many scriptures throughout the Bible that teach about prayer..."

So far, we have looked at two requirements for answered prayer—one being faith, "believing," and the other being that the prayer must be *"according to His will."* Both requirements are necessary, and one without the other simply won't cut it. Furthermore, John 15:7 states, *"if you remain in me and my word remains in you, ask whatever you wish and it will be done for you."* Right here, a person may focus on—whether consciously or subconsciously—the *"ask whatever you wish"* portion of the scripture. However, this scripture is clearly conditional. In other words, the second portion of the sentence is dependent upon the first portion of the sentence—"dependent clause"— meaning that a person must "remain in [Christ] and [His word (Christ's Word) must] remain in [a person in order for that person to be able to] *ask whatever* [he or she may] *wish, and it will be done for* [him or her.]" Therefore, a person must remain in Christ in order to *"ask whatever* [they] *wish,"* and for *"it* [to] *be done for* [them"]. Now that we have looked at three different requirements from three different scriptures and three different *pages,* let's take a quick look at Matthew 18:19-20 which states, *"again I say to you that if two of you agree on earth concerning anything that they ask, it will be done for them by My Father in heaven. For where to or three are gathered together in My name, I am there in the midst of them."*

> *"For where to or three are gathered together in My name, I am there in the midst of them."* (Matthew 18:20)

Here we see that if two people agree about the same thing in prayer, God will give them what they're asking for. Does this now mean that all I have to do in order to get a prayer answered is find someone who will agree with me and then pray together—absolutely not. One scripture does not nullify another, nor does one promise from God nullify a separate promise from God. Simply put, the requirement in John 15:7 still remains—which means that both individuals who have *agreed* together and are praying together, still must [both] *"remain in* [Christ],"* and Christ's Word must remain in them. In addition, to *remaining in* Christ and Christ's Word Remaining in them, they both also must *believe* and be praying for something that is *"according to His Will."*

(Simply for the sake of clarity, *individual prayer* still has a lot of power by itself, and God will answer your *individual prayer.* In other words, *individual prayer* is NOT dependent upon agreement with another person; however, the person who prays by his or her *self* must still *believe—remain in Christ, and His word must remain in [him or her]*—and the person must be praying (asking) for something that is *according to His Will.* The purpose of praying with someone else in *agreement* is that it does not simply *double* the power of the prayer, but it actually *multiplies* it. *"One will put 1,000 to flight; two will put 10,000 to flight, when God is on our side"* (Deuteronomy 32:30). This is simply one method that increases the power of prayer; another is adding *fasting* to your prayer. There is a story in the Bible when Jesus's disciples tried to heal a boy with epilepsy, but could not do so, so Jesus— after healing the boy—said to his disciples, "however, this kind does not go out except by prayer and fasting" (Matthew 17:21 KJV). Slight digression but absolutely necessary)

As a result of looking at some of the above mentioned scriptures, what have we learned? We have learned that in order for our prayers to be answered, we must:

1.) Believe.

2.) Remain in Christ, and His word must remain in us.

3.) Pray prayers that are according to His Will.

4.) Pray in agreement (not disagreement) with another believer/ Christian

And, any *one* of these four without *one* of the other 3, simply will not work alone.

Question: in your opinion, if the owner's manual states that you will get 336 "city miles" per gallon or 480 "highway miles" per gallon, and you fill the tank up with the best gasoline, but do not add any of the other four elements—1.) oil, 2.) transmission fluid, 3.) antifreeze 4.) air— do you believe that you will still get the expected miles per gallon? Moreover, would you then come to the conclusion that the car manual is inaccurate or misleading? Probably not.

> *"This is simply another example of how AWESOME God is to us…"*

Lastly, regarding this subject of prayer—and turning the page—there are some exceptions. For instance, Mark 9:23-25 states, "'*If you can'? said Jesus. 'Everything is possible for one who believes.' Immediately the boy's father exclaimed, 'I do believe; help me overcome my unbelief!' When Jesus saw that the crowd was running to the scene, he rebuked the impure spirit. 'You deaf and mute spirit,' He said, 'I command you, come out of him and never enter him again.'*" And the boy was healed. Now, to some, this may seem like a contradiction. However, in this situation, the boy's father admits his *unbelief* (lack of faith) to Jesus, and Jesus still decides to heal his son. This is simply another example of how AWESOME God is to us—that, even when we don't quite measure up (in our faith), He still decides to display His mercy and grace by healing the man's son, despite his lack of faith. In addition, Romans 9:15 states, "For he says to Moses, 'I will have mercy on whom I choose to have mercy, and I will have compassion on whom I choose to have compassion." In other words, the final decision is always up to God.

One might say, "well Nick, in that case, why bother to pray at all?" Because many find great comfort and confidence knowing that they are praying according to God's "guidelines." Simply put, who do you think experiences more answered prayer, the person who prays to God according to His *guidelines*, or the person who does not pray at all?

THE END